THE AMAZING BOOK OF PEOPLE

THE AMAZING BOOK OF FIRSTS
PEOPLE

Written by David Smith & Sue Cassin

Illustrated by Kim Blundell

Edited by Catriona Macgregor

COLLINS

CONTENTS

OCCUPATIONS
p. 6-7

All about the first people in various occupations, from lion tamers to the first disc jockey.

ROYALTY
p. 8-9

How the world's Kings and Queens have achieved regal firsts, from motoring monarchs to regal high heels.

MONEY MATTERS
p. 10-11

Where the first coins were issued, why paper notes were invented, and other financial firsts.

INDIVIDUAL SPORTS
p. 12-13

The origins of golf, tennis and many other individual sports that have been played for centuries.

TEAM SPORTS
p. 14-15

Where and when all sorts of popular team sports, from football to ice hockey, were developed.

ENTERTAINMENT
p. 16-17

The first zoo, circus, feature film and other achievements from the world of entertainment.

COSMETICS
p. 18-19

Who wore the first eyeshadow? When was lipstick first used? Find out the answers to these and other cosmetic questions.

CLOTHES
p. 20-21

Facts about all sorts of clothes, from the first swimsuit to the first pair of jeans.

ABOUT BABIES
p. 22-23

Including such firsts as the winner of the first baby show, the first pram and the first baby to be born in Antarctica.

CHILDREN'S SPECIAL
p. 24-25

All about places and events that involve children, such as the first playground and the first child Pope!

WRITERS AND MUSICIANS
p. 26-27

A selection of some of the many firsts about famous authors and composers.

FIGHTING CRIME
p. 28-29

Firsts from the world of crime and detection, from the burglar alarm to the first doggy detective agency!

OCCUPATIONS

BRAVE SHOWMAN—'Manchester Jack' was the first lion tamer. He was in charge of the lions at Wombwell's Menageria, a travelling show that toured England during the nineteenth century.

MODEL MRS—Marie Worth of the Paris fashion house Maison Gagelin et Opigez was the first fashion model. In 1852 she began modelling dresses designed by her husband Charles Frederick Worth.

FIRST FOOT MAN—The first chiropodist was David Low of London, England. He began 'corn cutting' in 1780 and by 1785 he had written about the foot.

FIRST CHAUFFEUR—Edward Thompson of Worthing, England, became the first chauffeur in June 1895. He drove a Panhard Levassor car for the Hon. Evelyn Ellis.

FEARLESS FLYER—Lieutenant H.H. Arnold was the first film stuntman. In September 1911 he performed the flying sequences in a film called 'The Military Air Scout' at Nassau Boulevard, New York.

CANNON CAREER—The first person to be fired from a cannon was a lady called 'Zazel'. She began her unusual job in April 1877 at West's Amphitheatre in London.

RADIO RECORD—Christopher Stone was the first disc jockey. He presented a record round-up for the BBC in London on 7 July, 1927.

FIRST TRAPEZE MAN—In 1859 Jules Leotard performed the first flying-trapeze act in Paris. His name is given to the leotard costume, still worn by acrobats and gymnasts.

ROYALTY

FIRST PILOT—The Infante Don Alfonso of Orleans and Bourbon, a cousin of King Alfonso of Spain, was the first royal person to qualify as a pilot. He learned to fly on an Antoinette monoplane in France in 1910.

WAR ON FLEAS—The first (and only) monarch to declare war on fleas was Queen Christina of Sweden. In 1658 she used a miniature cannon to fire tiny cannon balls at fleas she saw.

DOGGY BATH—In 1837 Victoria became Queen of Great Britain and her first proclamation was that each of her eighty pet dogs was to be given a bath.

BLUSHING QUEEN—Cleopatra, Queen of Egypt in 50 BC, was the first queen to rouge her cheeks. She used red ochre, a mixture made from clay.

TALL TALE—King Louis of France, known as the Sun King, reigned from 1643 to 1715. He was the first person, male or female, to wear high heels.

ROYAL LOO—The first monarch to use a w.c. was the English Queen Elizabeth I. It was designed by Sir John Havington, a poet, and was fitted at Richmond Palace in 1596.

FATTEST KING—The first monarch known to weigh over 200kg was the 1.9m tall King Taufa'ahau of Tonga. In 1976 he scaled 209.5kg.

FIRST SUB TRIP—In 1624 King James I of Britain was a passenger on the first submarine, which was built by Cornelius Drebbel, a Dutchman. The submarine was being demonstrated in the River Thames and was manned by twelve rowers, whose oars stuck out through sealed ports.

MOTORING MONARCH—The first royal motorist was the Sultan of Turkey, who drove an electric car in 1888. It had room for four people and reached a speed of 16km/h. The Sultan of Morocco was the first monarch to own a petrol-driven car. In 1892 he bought a four-wheel Canstatt Daimler.

MONEY MATTERS

COIN ISSUE—Kings Gyges of Lydia, which is now part of Turkey, issued the first coins between 690 and 650 BC. They were roughly cast of electrum, a natural mixture of gold and silver. Trade was growing rapidly in the Mediterranean area, so other countries soon started to use coins.

MERCHANTS' BANK—Jewish merchants began the first bank in Lombardy, Italy, in AD 808.

PAPER NOTES—The first paper money was issued by Emperor Hein Tsung in China between AD 806 and 821, due to a shortage of coins.

CHEQUE AUCTION—In April 1659 the London bankers, Clayton and Morris, handled the first known cheque. It was for the sum of £10. In 1976 the same cheque was sold by auction at Sotheby's in London for £1,300.

MOBILE MONEY—In 1892 the first mobile bank was operated on the Palmerston-Otaki railway in North Island, New Zealand.

CAR CRIME—The first bank hold-up in which cars were used was by the Jules Bonnot gang in December 1911 when they robbed the Société Générale Bank in Paris.

SAFETY CHEQUE—Robert Herries, a London banker, issued the first traveller's cheques in January 1772. They could be used in 90 cities from Madrid to Moscow and were guaranteed against theft.

CREDIT CARD CLUB—Credit cards were first issued in the 1920s by oil companies in the USA. The first credit card for use in shops and hotels was brought out in 1950 by the Diners Club Inc. of the USA.

DRIVE-IN DEBIT—The first drive-in bank, the Exchange National Bank, was opened in 1946 in Chicago.

11

INDIVIDUAL SPORTS

BONESHAKER RACE—The first known cycle race took place in France in May 1868. About 100 competitors took part, all riding 'boneshaker' bicycles with iron rims. The race was won by an English doctor, James Moore, who covered the course at an average speed of just 11km/h.

The most famous cycle race of all, the Tour de France, was first staged in 1903. It lasts 25 days over a course of more than 4,000km.

BANNED SPORT—Golf was first played in the 15th century in Scotland. In fact, in 1457 it was banned by order of the Scottish Parliament because it was so popular that it kept men from important archery practice!

FEATHER GOLF BALL—The first golf balls were made of wood, but later they were made of feathers inside a leather cover. However, the rubber-cored ball, which is still used today, was not invented until 1899 and was the idea of an American dentist.

MONKS' TENNIS—In 1858 the first game of lawn tennis was played in Birmingham. The two competitors were Harry Gem and Guigurio Pevera. This popular game is based on 'real tennis', first played in French monasteries in about AD 1050.

The first tennis club was started in 1872 at Lemington Spa in England.

12

PING PONG HISTORY—Table tennis used to be known as 'gossima'. The game was devised in about 1881 by James Gibb from the UK, and was played using rubber balls. Next he used celluloid balls and called the game 'ping pong' because of the noise the ball made as it was hit back and forth on the table.

SKI CARVING—Skiing as a modern sport began in 1843, when a cross-country competition took place at Tromso, Norway. However, skiing is much older than that. In 1934 an ancient rock carving of a skier was discovered at Bessovysledki, USSR. It dates from about 6000 BC.

BONE ICE SKATES—The first ice skates were made of animal bones. They were found in France and are thought to be as old as 20,000 years.

The first report of skating as a sport is in a British chronicle dated 1175, but the first club was formed much later in Edinburgh in 1742.

BOXING BUTCHER—The British Duke of Albermarle organised the first boxing match in January 1681. It took place between the Duke's butler and his butcher!

Modern boxing began in 1867. The Marquess of Queensbury introduced strict rules which, in a modified form, are still in use today.

SPEEDY SWIMMER—Until the 19th century most people swam using the breast stroke and it wasn't until the early 20th century that the American swimmer, Johnny Weissmüller, developed what is known today as the front crawl.

TEAM SPORTS

BASKETBALL ORIGINS—A game similar to basketball was played in Mexico in the 10th century, but today's basketball sport was devised in December 1891 by Canadian-born Dr James Naismith in Massachusetts. The first game was played in January 1892.

SUMMER SPORT—Baseball was first played in England in around 1700. However, the first game played under modern rules (Cartwright rules) took place at Hoboken, New Jersey in the summer of 1846.

FOOTBALL FIRST—American football was developed at American universities in the 19th century. The first match under the Harvard rules was played between the Harvard and McGill Universities in 1874.

SOCCER SUCCESS—There was a Chinese ball-kicking game called *Tsu-chin* which was played in about 350 BC, but the first modern rules were made at Cambridge University, England, in 1846. It is now played in most countries and is the world's most popular sport.

EASY OPTION—Volleyball was devised in 1895 by William Morgan, an American YMCA instructor at Holyoke, Massachusetts, as a game for those who 'found basketball too strenuous'. The name 'volleyball' was suggested by Dr Holsted of Springfield in 1896.

ICE EVENT—*Kalv*, a game very similar to ice hockey, was played in Holland in the sixteenth century. Modern ice hockey began at Christmas 1855 in Ontario, Canada. English soldiers played on ice with hockey sticks and a kind of puck.

EGYPTIAN HOCKEY—Hockey began many centuries ago. An Egyptian tomb dating from about 2050 BC has a painting showing two players with curved sticks and a ball.

15

ENTERTAINMENT

ANIMALS ON SHOW—From about 2095 BC onwards private collections of animals were kept—mainly for study—in the Middle East. These could be called the first zoos.

The first public zoo was at the Jardin des Plantes in Paris, France. It was opened in June 1793.

BALLET FIRST—Ballet performances originally included speech and song. The first ballet to be performed using only mime and gestures was John Weaver's *The Loves of Mars and Venus*. It was presented at the Theatre Royal in Drury Lane, London, in 1717.

CIRCUS RING—In London in 1769 an ex-Cavalry sergeant-major called Philip Hotley established the first circus. He sold a diamond ring, which he found on Westminster Bridge, to cover the cost of the show.

Charlie Revel of Spain was the oldest clown—he performed for 82 years (1899–1981).

SHIPWRECK SCENE—People could view seascapes for the first time without going underwater when the oceanarium, 'Marineland of Florida', was opened in the USA in 1938. Up to 26.3 million litres of sea water were pumped each day through two huge tanks. Inside the tanks spectators could see natural sea scenes, including coral reefs and even a shipwreck.

FILM FEATURES—In 1895 the Lumière Brothers showed their films at the world's first public cinema screen in Paris, France.

People had to wait until 1914 to see the first full-length feature film in natural colour. It was called *The World, the Flesh and the Devil* and was made in the UK.

RECORD SALES—The world's biggest selling gramophone record is 'White Christmas', written by Irving Berlin. It has sold over 170 million copies in various recordings.

The Beatles were the first pop group to sell more than 1,000 million records and cassette tapes.

THRILLER PLAY—*The Mousetrap*, adapted from an Agatha Christie thriller, is the world's first play to run continuously for as long as 37 years. It opened in London in 1952 and has so far been seen by more than 7 million people.

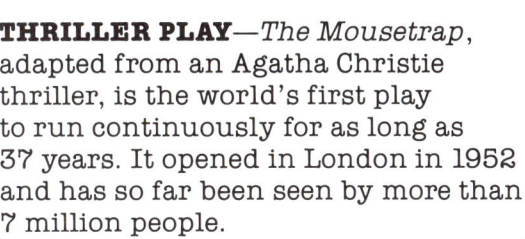

ROCK RECORD—Rock music dates from the early 1950s. The term 'rock and roll' was first applied to the songs 'Rock Around the Clock' (by Bill Hayley and the Comets) and 'Heartbreak Hotel' (by Elvis Presley).

COSMETICS

SKIN SAVERS—In about 7500 BC Egyptian shepherds and hunters in the Nile Valley were the first people to use a preparation to protect their skin. The oil, from crushed castor beans, was rubbed into the skin.

BEAUTY AND THE BEES—The first cold cream was made in AD 200 by a Greek doctor called Galen. It was a mixture of beeswax oil and olive oil. Today's cold cream is more or less the same mixture.

PAINTED QUEEN—Queen Nefertiti of Egypt, in 1370 BC, was the first person to paint her fingernails and toenails ruby red—a colour only royalty were allowed to use at that time.

PATENT POLISH—In 1916 the first liquid nail polish, Cutex, was produced in the USA.

ANCIENT BEAUTY AIDS—Women in Ancient Greece (750 BC) were the first to dye their hair (black) and put face make-up on their skin (white lead powder).

EYE DYE—The Romans in 150 BC were the first people to use eye make-up. They painted gold around their eyes and used woodash to blacken their eyelids.

EYE EXTRAS—False eyelashes were first worn in 1916 by an American actress called Seena Owen, in the film *Intolerance*.

LIPSTICK LINER—The first mass-produced lipstick in metal containers was made by Maurice Levy in the USA, in 1915.

19

CLOTHES

PHARAOH FOOTWEAR—The first shoes are thought to have been leather sandals, worn in Egypt in about 1500 BC.

SMELLY SUCCESS—In 1823 a Scottish chemist, Charles Macintosh, made the first waterproof coats, still known to this day as 'macintoshes'. At first, people weren't very keen on them because they were supposed to have had a peculiar smell.

JEAN GENIUS—In 1850 Levi Strauss, a German immigrant to San Francisco, made the first pair of jeans. They were produced as hard-wearing work trousers for the Gold Rush miners. The new trousers were called 'jeans' because the cloth was first made in Genoa, in Italy, and the French name for that city is 'Genes'.

WELLIE WONDER—Rubber wellington boots were first made by the North British Rubber Company of Edinburgh in 1865. The boots were named after the Duke of Wellington.

BIKINI BOMBSHELL—In July 1946 a dancer called Micheline Bernardi became the first person to wear a bikini. She modelled it at a Paris fashion show four days after an atomic bomb test had been carried out at Bikini Atoll in the Pacific Ocean—hence the name 'bikini'.

SWIMSUIT SCANDAL—Before the 1900s swimmers used to wear combinations which covered their arms and legs. In 1909 Annette Kellerman wore the first swimsuit with trousers ending 4cm above the knees and sleeves just covering her shoulders. Nevertheless she was arrested for 'indecent exposure'.

MINI-MAKER—The mini-skirt was designed by Mary Quant, an English designer, and was first worn in 1965—about 15cm above the knees.

COWBOY HAT—The first 'western' or '10 gallon hat' was made in 1866 by an American, John Stetson.

LADY IN TROUSERS—The French actress, Sarah Bernhardt, caused a stir in 1876 when she became the first woman to wear a pair of man's trousers in public. It was more than 30 years before it happened again!

ABOUT BABIES

NEW NAPPIES—'Paddipads' were the world's first disposable nappies. They were introduced in 1949 by Robinson's of Chesterfield in Great Britain.

INCUBATOR INVENTION—In 1891 a French doctor called Alexandre Lion devised the first baby incubator to help weak and premature babies.

ANTARCTIC BABY—The first baby to be born in Antarctica was Emilio Marcos Palma of Argentina, on 7 January 1978 at the Sargento Cabral Base.

BABY FACE—The first baby show ever was held at Springfield, Ohio, USA, in 1854. The winner was the 10-month-old baby of Mr and Mrs W. Romner, Ohio.

SHELL-SHAPED PRAM—William Kent built the first pram ever in about 1733. It was made at Chatsworth in England for the third Duke of Devonshire. The pram was fitted with wheels which were 52cm in diameter at the rear and 40cm in diameter at the front. The body of the pram was in the shape of a scallop shell and had a folding hood. Its undercarriage was made of bronze snakes! Shafts and a small collar were attached to the pram, so that it could be pulled by a dog.

FIRST QUINS—The first known quins to survive were Emilie, Yvonne, Cecile, Marie and Annette Dionne—born in Ontario, Canada, 28 May 1934.

The first known sextuplets to survive were 3 girls and 3 boys born to Mrs Sue Rosenkowitz of Cape Town, South Africa, on 11 January 1974.

BIRTHDAY BOOM—The first record of one family having 5 children with the same birthday is that of the Cummins family of Virginia, USA. The 5 children—Catherine (1952), Carol (1953), Charles (1956), Claudia (1961) and Cecilia (1966)—were all born on 20 February!

CHILDREN'S SPECIAL

TOY STORE BANK—In October 1988 the first children's bank opened in New York. The bank is inside Schwarz's toy store and has child-size teller booths, store debit cards and a cartoon book featuring the adventures of Denny Decimal, Debit the Frog, and Mr Greenback.

CHILDREN'S LIBRARY—The first children's library opened in January 1803, in Salisbury, Connecticut. It was started by a bookseller called Calib Bingham and had a stock of 150 books. It was intended for the exclusive use of children aged 9 to 16 years.

RADIO SERIES—*The Man in the Moon Stories for Children* was the first regular children's radio programme. It was broadcast twice-weekly from Westinghouse's WJZ station, Newark, New Jersey, and began in the Autumn of 1921.

CHILDREN'S THEATRE—The first children's theatre was 'The Children's Educational Theater' in New York. It opened in October 1903 with a production of Shakespeare's *The Tempest*.

CHILDREN'S WARD—The first children's hospital ward was opened at Guy's Hospital in London in 1848.

FIRST PLAYGROUND—The first children's playground was opened in a municipal park in Manchester, in 1859. It was fitted with swings and horizontal bars.

CHILDREN'S CRUSADE—In 1212 a French farm boy called Stephen of Cloyes persuaded 30,000 children to set out on the first children's crusade, to the Holy Land from France. However, when they reached the port of Marseille they were lured onto ships and sold into slavery.

CHILD POPE—The first child to be elected as Pope was Benedict IX. He began his papacy in 1032, when he was only 12 years old, and he remained Pope for 14 years.

25

WRITERS AND MUSICIANS

MAGIC NOVELS—In 1841 the American author Edgar Alan Poe wrote the first modern detective thriller, *The Murders in the Rue Morgue*. He wrote his books with his black cat, Magic, sitting on his shoulder.

CHILD GENIUS—Mozart was probably the youngest successful composer. He wrote his first symphony in 1763 when he was only seven years old.

HIGH-PRICED PIANIST—The first to earn as much as $2 million, for just 26 weeks of work, was the American musician, Valentino Liberace.

BABY MUSICIAN—The youngest person to give an organ recital was William Crotch of Norwich, in 1778, when he was only three years old. A year later he was giving daily concert recitals in London.

PIGTAIL PLOY—When the Austrian composer, Joseph Haydn, was a choirboy in St Stephen's Cathedral, Vienna, he used scissors to cut off the pigtail of the boy in front of him. He was expelled immediately, but he went on to become the first person to write more than 100 symphonies.

MYSTERY WRITER—The first author to receive over 740 rejections from publishers was John Creasey of the UK. Once his first book was published he continued writing and created a total of 564 mystery novels.

COMPOSER'S CASTLE—The German composer, Richard Wagner, was the first musician to have a castle built so that his operas could be performed in it. In 1874 King Ludwig II of Bavaria—a great fan of Wagner—built the fairytale-like castle of Neuschwanstein especially for him.

TORTOISE TALE—Aeschylus, a Greek poet who lived between 525 and 456 BC, was the first and only poet to be killed by a tortoise! According to legend an eagle was flying overhead, carrying a tortoise in its claws. The eagle mistook Aeschylus' bald head for a stone and dropped the tortoise onto the poet, killing him immediately.

FIGHTING CRIME

FULL-TIME DETECTIVE—The first police detective was a Frenchman called Eugène Francois Vidocq. He became head of the French Sureté in 1812 and was the first full-time member of a regular police force to specialize in detective work.

INTERNATIONAL CRIME—Interpol, the first international crime fighting organisation, was formed in 1923 at Paris headquarters. It has an international criminal register and fingerprint file.

BIKE PATROL—The first police motorcycle patrol was begun in 1905 by the New York City police department. They bought three machines, which were so sucessful that they purchased a further twenty the following year.

DETECTIVE DOG—The first time a specially trained dog was used in the arrest of criminals was in Aberdeenshire, Scotland. In 1816 a Revenue Officer and his bull-terrier caught a gang of whisky smugglers. The dog bit their horses' noses, making them rear up, and the smugglers dropped their casks of whisky onto the ground!

NO. 1 WOMAN—A former social worker called Alice Wells became the first policewoman. She was appointed to the Los Angeles Police Department in 1910 and was issued with Policewoman's badge No. 1.

DOCTOR AT SEA—An American doctor called Henry Crippen was the first murderer to be arrested after a radio message was sent to a ship at sea. In 1910 he thought that he had succeeded in escaping from England on board *SS Montrose*, which was en route for Canada. However, police sent a message alerting the ship's Captain.

STUBBORN STILTWALKER—The first (and possibly only) time a policeman handed out a summons wearing stilts was in the 1930s in La Paz, Bolivia. By law the summons had to be handed personally to a stiltwalker in a circus, but he wouldn't come down off his stilts! Two policemen then found some stilts, put them on and handed the surprised circus performer his summons.

BURGLAR SHOCK—The first electric burglar alarm was installed by Edwin Holmes of Boston, Massachusetts, in 1858.

INDEX

babies, 22–3
    baby show, 22
    incubator, 22
    nappies, 22
    pram, 23
    quintuplets, 23
    sextuplets, 23
ballet, 16
banks, 10–11, 24
    drive-in, 11
    mobile, 11
baseball, 14
basketball, 14
boxing match, 13

chauffeur, 6
cheques, 10, 11
children, 24–5
    bank, 24
    crusade, 25
    hospital ward, 25
    library, 24
    playground, 25
    pope, 25
    radio series, 24
chiropodist, 6
circus, 16
clothes, 20–1
    bikini, 20
    cowboy hat, 21
    jeans, 20
    macintoshes, 20
    miniskirts, 21
    sandals, 20
    swimsuit, 21
    wellington boots, 20
    women's trousers, 21
coins, 10
cosmetics, 18–19
    cold cream, 18
    eye make-up, 19
    false eyelashes, 19
    hair dye, 19
    lipstick, 19
    nail polish, 18
credit cards, 11
crime, 28–9
    burglar alarm, 29
    detective, 28
    Interpol, 28
    motorcycle patrol, 28
    police dog, 28
    policewoman, 29
cycle race, 12

disc jockey, 7

football, American, 14

golf, 12
gramophone records, 17
    biggest selling, 17
    rock and roll, 17

high heels, 9
hockey, 15
human cannonball, 7

lion tamer, 6

model, 6
musicians, 26–7
    highest paid pianist, 26
    youngest composer, 26

pilot 8
ping pong, 13
plays, 17
    longest running, 17

rouge, 8
royalty, 8–9

skating, 13
skiing, 13
soccer, 14
sport, 12–15
stuntman, 7
submarine, 9
swimming, 13

tennis, 12
trapeze artist, 7
traveller's cheques, 11

w.c., 9
writers, 26–7
    detective stories, 26

zoos, 16

HAMLYN - COLOURF

FISHING

BRIAN MORLAND

CONTENTS

Equipment	2
Species	4
Casting	6
Float fishing	8
Spinning and deadbaiting	10
Fly fishing 1	12
Fly fishing 2	14
Legering	16
Rivers 1	18
Rivers 2	20
Lakes, ponds & gravel pits 1	22
Lakes, ponds & gravel pits 2	24
Canals	26
Seasons	28
Angler's Code	30
Index and glossary	32

HAMLYN

EQUIPMENT

Fishing is one of the most popular pastimes that can be enjoyed by anyone, regardless of age. For the young angler, it can provide an opportunity to learn about wildlife and the environment.

There is usually a bewildering array of rods in any shop selling fishing tackle, but basically there are only two types of rod for coarse fishing. One is the three piece match or float fishing rod, and the other is the shorter two section leger rod. Eventually you will need at least two rods but if you can only afford one to begin with then choose the larger float rod. A 3.7 metre three piece carbon or glass rod is ideal for beginners.

When choosing a leger rod think carefully about where you are going to do most of your fishing. Be guided by an expert in the tackle shop. Once you have bought a good rod and reel then gradually you can build up other items such as floats.

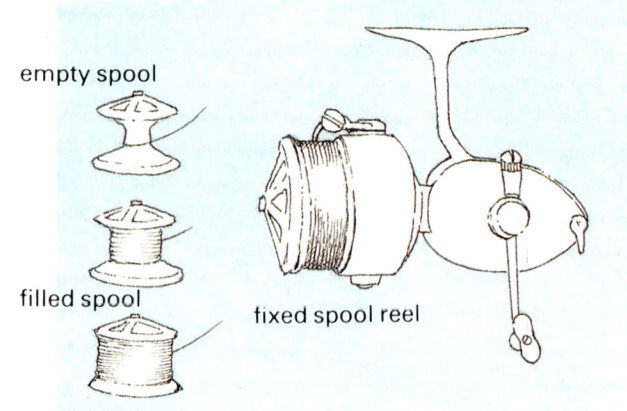

Reels There are two main types of fixed spool reel. In a closed face fixed spool reel the spool is enclosed in a metal housing and line is fed out through the front of this housing. A press button release mechanism allows one handed casting. In a standard fixed spool reel, the spool is exposed at the front of the reel.

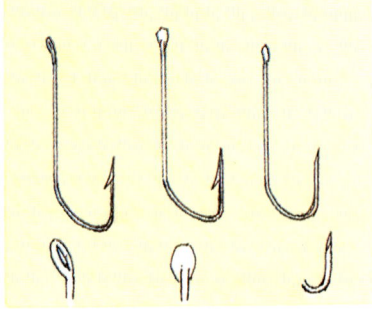

eyed   spade end   barbless

Hooks The size of hook is determined by its number; the higher the number, the smaller the hook. A size 16 or 18 is right for fishing maggots and casters. Use a size 8 or larger for big baits. Barbless hooks are now preferred by most anglers.

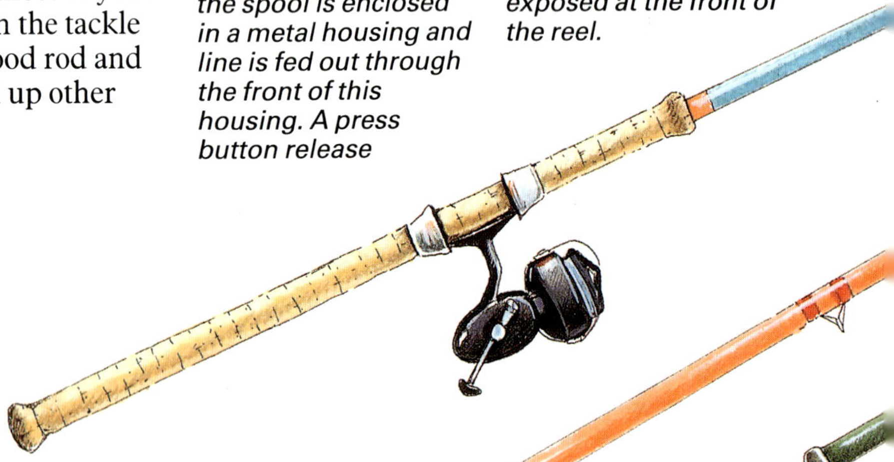

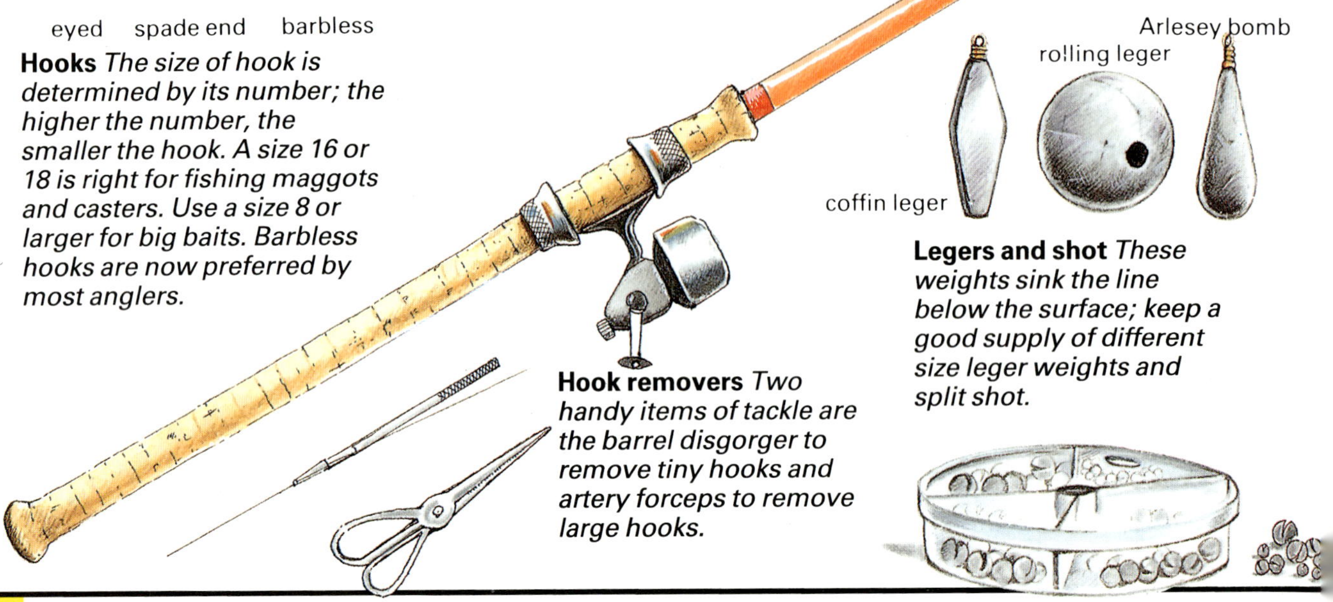

coffin leger

Arlesey bomb
rolling leger

Legers and shot These weights sink the line below the surface; keep a good supply of different size leger weights and split shot.

Hook removers Two handy items of tackle are the barrel disgorger to remove tiny hooks and artery forceps to remove large hooks.

Keepnets and rests *Choose the most spacious keepnet you can afford and make sure the mesh is knotless. Landing nets come in triangular and circular forms. It is easier to extract fish from flat-bottomed pan nets.*

Bags and seats *A rucksack or a canvas tackle bag is an essential. A light, fold-up chair is the ideal, portable fishing seat.*

It is important that when the line is wound onto the reel it should end up 1.5 millimetres below the front rim of the spool. If the spool is a deep one, wind backing line on first.

Bait *Maggots, bread, cheese and worms are all excellent baits.*

Fishing line *Nylon line is bought in spools of 100 metres. What breaking strain (the weight a line will hold before snapping) you use depends on the size of fish you are hoping to catch. For float fishing a reel line of 1.4 kg is adequate.*

Floats *A good selection of stick, waggler and antenna floats will cover most circumstances.*

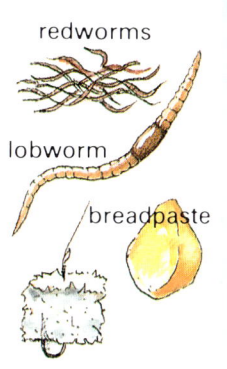

maggot
caster
cheesepaste
redworms
lobworm
breadpaste
breadflake

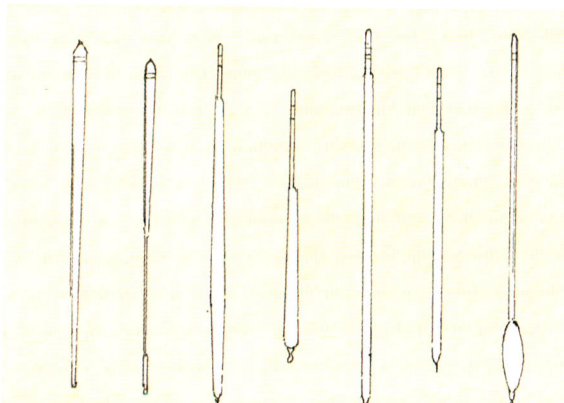

Rod action *Rods with just a tip action (where only the end section bends when playing fish) are best used for small species of fish. For bigger fish such as chub and barbel a rod with a through action is better.*

SPECIES

The most widespread species of fish in rivers are chub, dace and roach. **Chub** and **dace** are widespread throughout the length of a river and can even be found in the upper trout reaches. **Roach** numbers were much reduced by a disease several years ago and they disappeared from many waters, but they have since made a comeback and are found in most rivers. **Bream**, where they are to be found, are often very numerous and tend to move around in big shoals. Roach and bream often hybridise so it is interesting to check whether your catch is in fact a roach or a roach/bream hybrid.

Barbel are not as widely distributed as other species but in recent years they have been introduced to more rivers. In some, they have thrived to such an extent that they have ousted the chub as the main species. Another recent introduction to river life is the **zander** which has now colonised most lowland rivers and drainage ditches in eastern England.

The **carp** is probably the most sought after species in lakes. There are three types of king carp. The fully scaled fish is known as the common carp; the mirror carp has a very smooth skin apart from a row of very large

scales along its back and lateral line; the leather carp is totally scaleless. The small, fully-scaled crucian carp is a different species and has no barbules.

Tench are a summer species-fish which become inactive during winter. They are strong fighters. The male tench has huge, spoonlike pelvic fins. During the winter, tench become torpid and are seldom caught. **Perch** thrive in lakes and ponds and are prolific breeders. They are a hard-fighting species and always shoal close to some form of cover. They feed on tiny fish but will be tempted by a worm or maggot. **Eels** find their way along ditches into lakes and because there is no easy route back to the sea they can live there a long time and increase greatly in size. **Pike** are found in most lakes and ponds where they feed on anything from fish to baby ducklings.

perch

carp

tench

pike

CASTING

Casting is a skill which takes time and much practice to perfect. Casting with a fixed spool reel is fairly easy but remember that accuracy is more important than distance. Before fishing make sure that the reel is correctly filled with line. A badly-filled reel spool is the most common cause of casting difficulties.

A reel is usually supplied with two spools. There is a deep spool for heavy line and a shallow spool for fine line. If the line is wound on so that it is flush with the lip, it will fall off in coils and tangle. If the gap to the lip is too great then the line will not cast smoothly.

fixed spool reel with the bale arm open. Line to run off freely

Casting should be smooth and easy. If you have to force the line off the spool, check that the spool is correctly filled. For casting short distances there is no need to hold the butt of the rod.

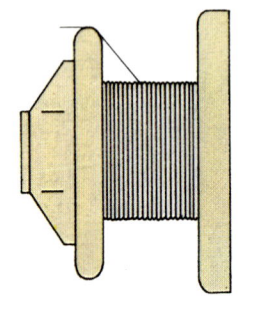

an underfilled spool can cause casting difficulties

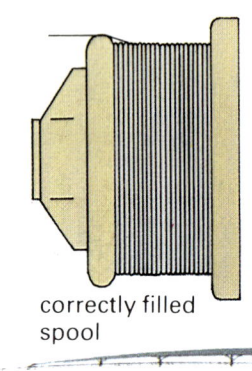

correctly filled spool

With the bale arm open, trap the line against the rim of the spool with your forefinger, then raise your arm back over your shoulder.

Bring the rod forward sharply and release the line.

The most widely-used method of casting is the overhead or overarm cast. The reel should be located near the top of the handle. Hold the rod just above the reel. Open the bale arm of the reel and trap the line against the rim of the spool. Hold the butt of the rod with your other hand and bring the rod back over your shoulder. To cast, push forward with the hand near the reel and pull back with the other hand. As the rod moves forward from the vertical position release the line. Follow through with the rod so it ends up slightly below the horizontal position. Engage the bale arm and tighten up to the float.

The bale arm should be engaged and the float tightened up.

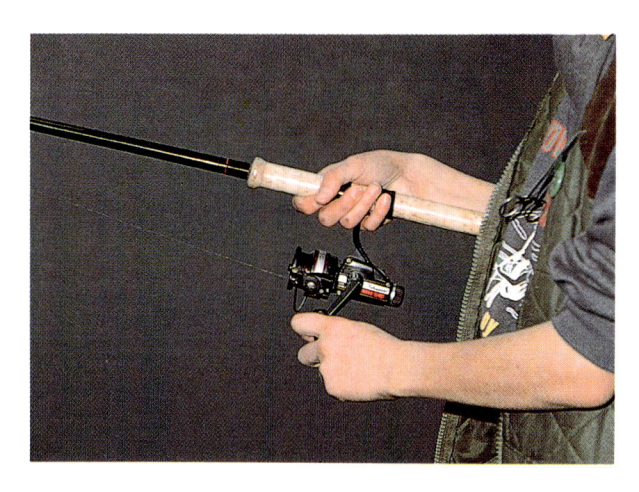

When you bring your rod back to make a cast make sure that the banking is not too steep or that the branches of trees will not tangle your line. Always beware of overhead cables.

Float fishing

Float fishing is one of the most popular and rewarding methods of fishing. A float has two main functions: most importantly, it is a bite indicator which tells when a fish has taken your bait. Secondly, by using different floats you can present a bait to the fish at different depths and in different ways. Tackle shops have many different shapes and colours of float to choose from and will give you expert advice on what to select.

It is an exciting moment when the float trembles and then disappears below the surface, and once mastered, float fishing is arguably the most skilful method of coarse fishing.

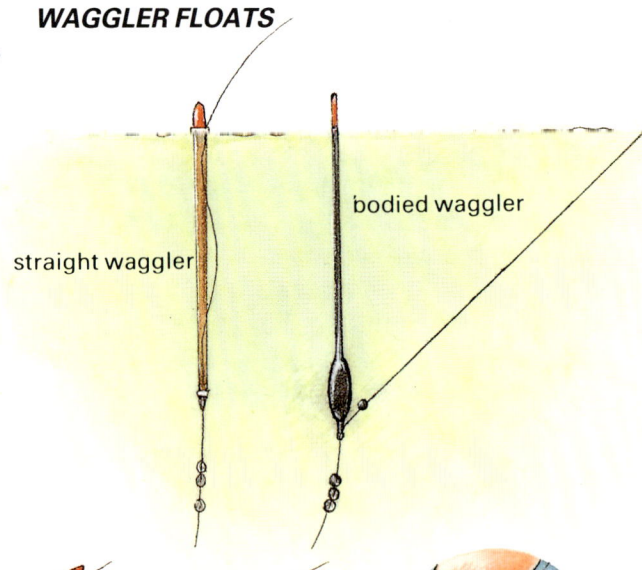

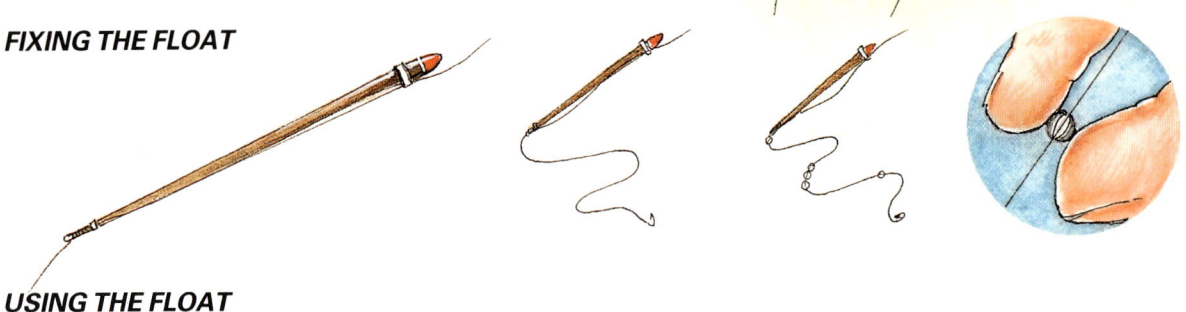

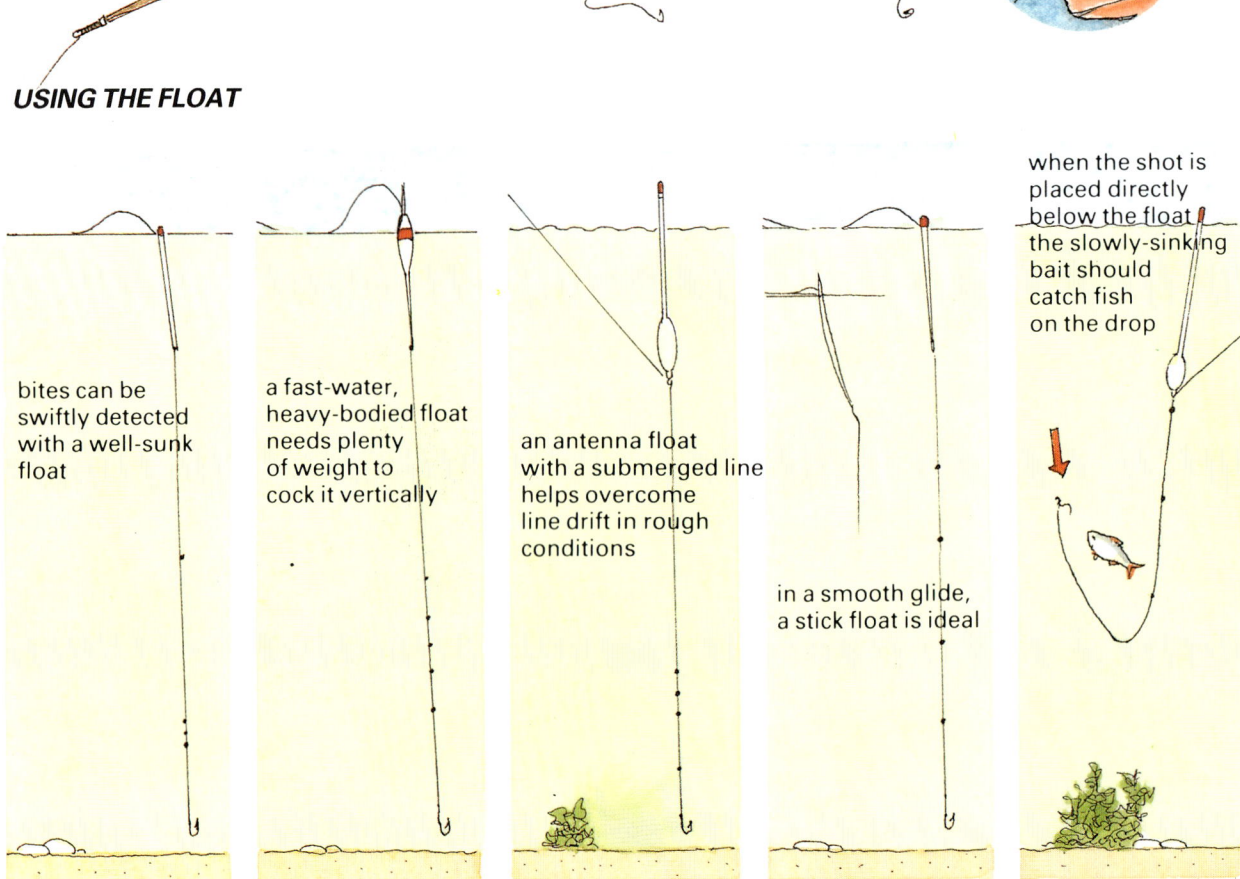

WAGGLER FLOATS

straight waggler

bodied waggler

FIXING THE FLOAT

USING THE FLOAT

bites can be swiftly detected with a well-sunk float

a fast-water, heavy-bodied float needs plenty of weight to cock it vertically

an antenna float with a submerged line helps overcome line drift in rough conditions

in a smooth glide, a stick float is ideal

when the shot is placed directly below the float the slowly-sinking bait should catch fish on the drop

TROTTING

Cast your float across the river and allow it to travel down the path of the current. This is called trotting.

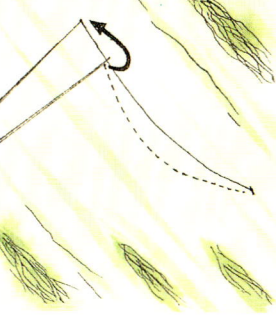

When trotting a long way, hold the rod high and mend the belly in the line by rolling the rod tip.

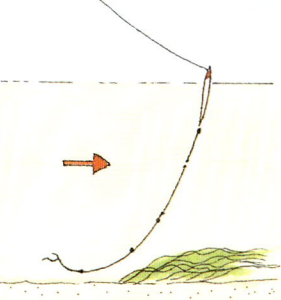

When allowed to travel at the speed of the current the float will always precede the bait.

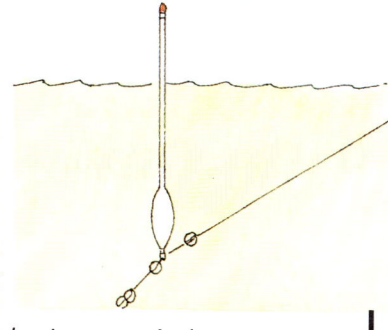

In very windy conditions use a long antenna float and undershot so more of the float is visible.

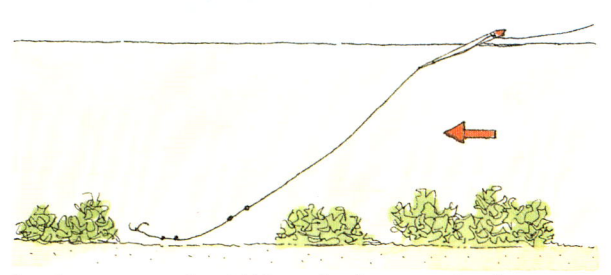

Laying on method When laying on, the float should be fixed to the reel line at the top and bottom with float rubbers. Set the float well over deep water. Cast across and downstream so that the current swings the tackle round until it comes to rest immediately downstream from your rod.

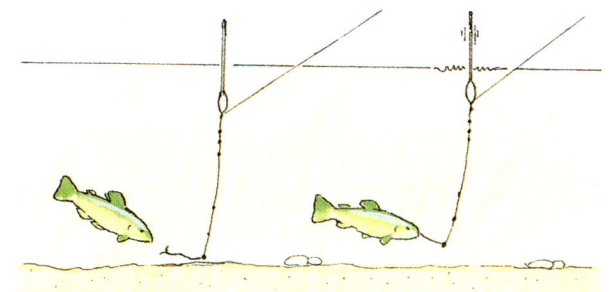

Lift method Plumb the depth very accurately and set the float so that the tip is just visible when the bottom shot is lying on the water's bed. When a fish picks up the bait the float will rise up in the water.

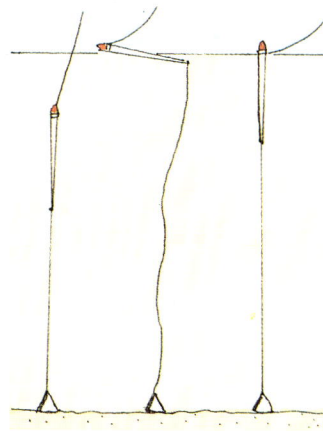

Setting the float Tie a heavy weight or plummet to the end of your line. If the float sinks, increase the distance of the weight from the float. The correct depth is achieved when the tip of the float touches the surface and the weight is on the river bed.

When to strike The classic bite on float tackle is when the float goes under and sails away. Often this doesn't happen, however, when the fish are sluggish. Fish will very often take a bait and not swim away and so register only slight movement on the float. Strike at any positive movement.

SPINNING AND DEADBAITING

Spinning and deadbaiting are used to catch the more predatory species of fish like pike, perch and zander. In spinning, the artificial lure is cast out, allowed to sink and then retrieved so that it wobbles or revolves to attract the fish. Eels will fall to small deadbaits and other species, notably chub, are also not averse to taking a spinner or deadbait. Big trout and even the dainty grayling will take a mepps spinner.

Pike are the most sought after predator fish and because they grow so large and have a vicious set of teeth, special tactics are needed. The rod needs to have a test curve of around 1 kg and a strong line of at least 5.4 kg (12 lb) breaking strain needs to be used. Deadbaits can be fished in three separate ways: they can be cast out and left on the bottom with the reel bale arm open for when the pike runs with the bait. A more active method is the sink and draw. The third way is to let the bait drift around under a float.

A pike is a fighter and will often leap clear.

Sea fish such as sprats, herring and mackerel make excellent deadbaits.

A spoon revolves and flashes as it is retrieved.

Deadbaits should be mounted on a wire trace at least 0.5 metres long situated between the hook and reel line. This prevents the teeth of the pike from biting through. The reel line is fastened to a swivel at the end of the trace. Two treble hooks can be used, preferably barbless.

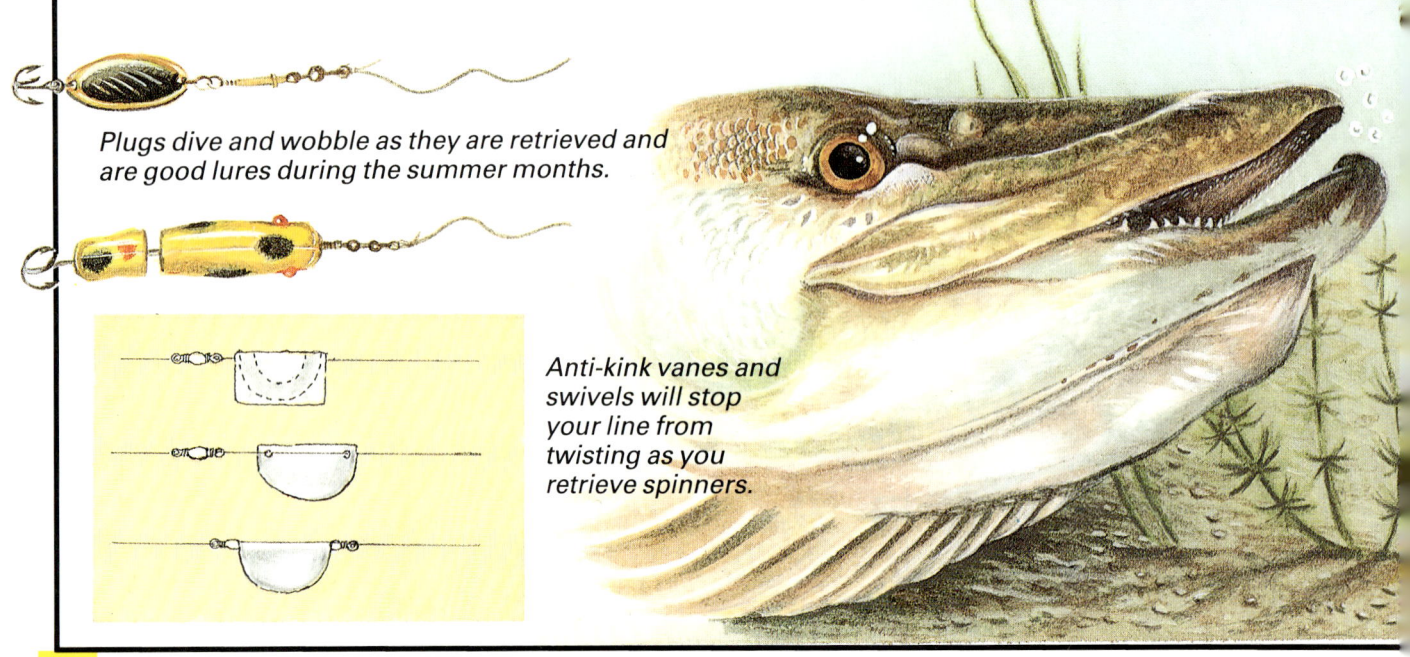

Plugs dive and wobble as they are retrieved and are good lures during the summer months.

Anti-kink vanes and swivels will stop your line from twisting as you retrieve spinners.

In the sink and draw *method, cast out the deadbait and allow it to flutter down through the water. Lift the rod and reel in sharply so that the bait moves forward and rises at the same time.*

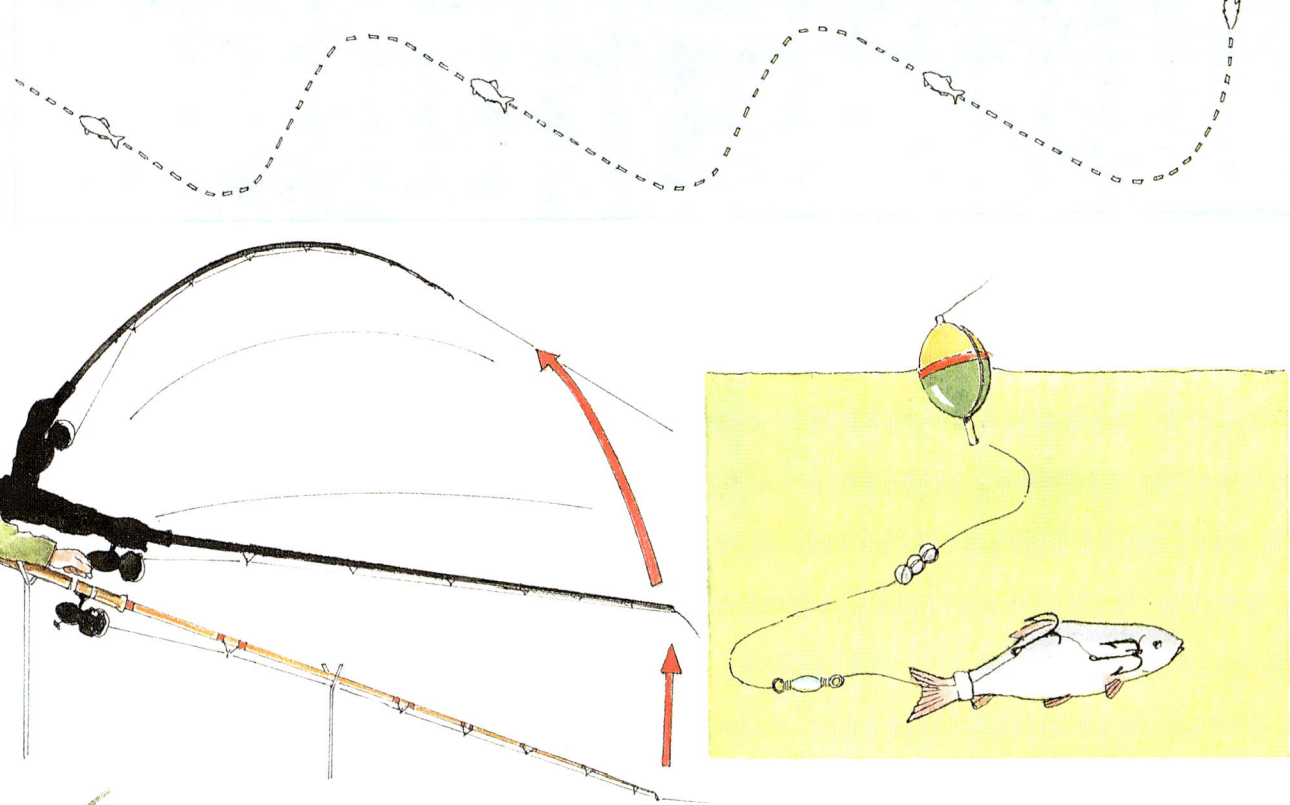

Striking *When you get a run on your deadbait, lift the rod from the rest and close the bale arm of the reel. Tighten up on the fish and then drive the hooks home with a solid sideways strike. Make sure the clutch has been set correctly to give plenty of line if the pike is exceptionally large.*

Float fished deadbait *When choosing a pike float ignore the traditional pike bungs and choose a modern streamlined pike float which offers less resistance to a taking fish. Set the depth so that the bait is clear of the bottom and let it drift in the wind or flow.*

Using a pike gag *Pike have extremely sharp teeth and so need to be handled carefully. To remove the hooks, lay the pike on a damp towel and if necessary kneel astride it to stop it jumping about. Insert the gag inside the pike's mouth to keep the jaws apart. Use a pair of long-nosed artery forceps to carefully remove the hooks. After weighing, release the pike straight back into the water.*

Pike gags have sharp forked ends. Protect yourself and the pike by tipping them with cork pads.

FLY FISHING 1

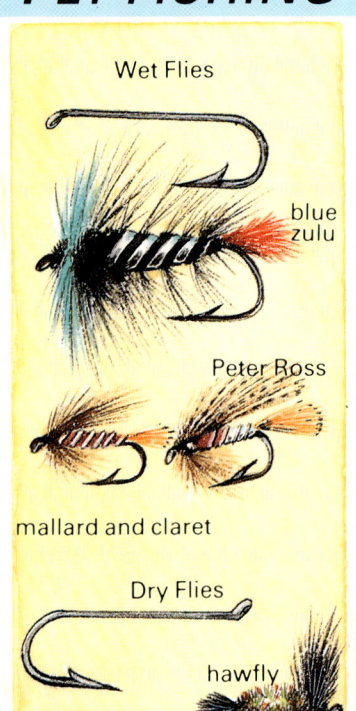

Wet Flies Wet flies are artificial flies tied with soft hackles that sink and imitate small insects or fly larvae.

blue zulu

Peter Ross

mallard and claret

Dry Flies These imitate emerging or land-borne insects. A dry fly has stiff hackles and stands off the surface film.

hawfly

mayfly

daddy long legs

Fly fishing is fishing with an artificial fly or lure instead of deadbait. Stillwater fly fishing for rainbow trout has become very popular in recent years. Many supply reservoirs have been opened up to trout fishing and there are hundreds of smaller commercial trout fisheries. Some young anglers are deterred from taking up fly fishing because they think it is too difficult, but in fact fly fishing is no more difficult than bait fishing for coarse fish. There is also the added bonus that you can eat your catch, unlike fish caught when coarse fishing.

Reels Choose as lightweight a reel as possible. Wind 25 metres of backing line onto the reel before winding on the actual fly line. This allows you to play a really big trout that strips all your fly line off the reel.

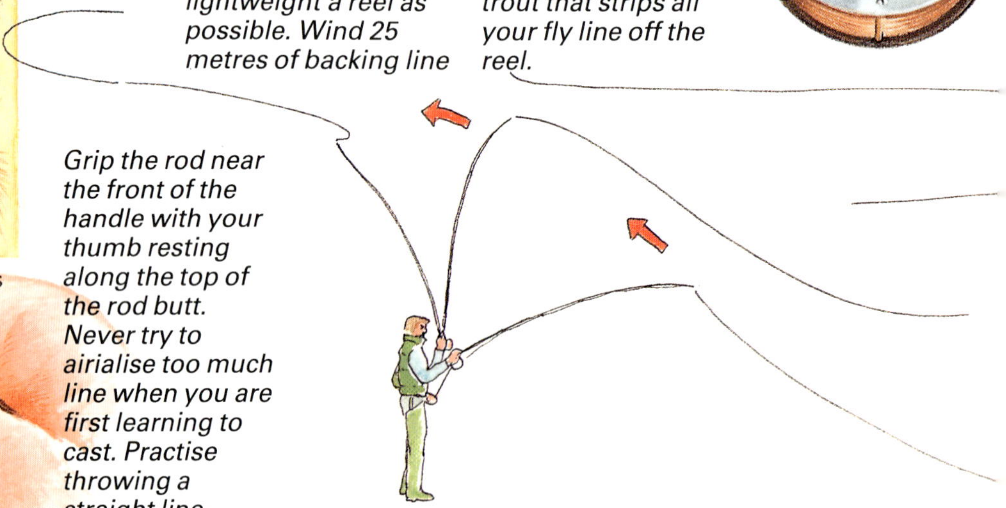

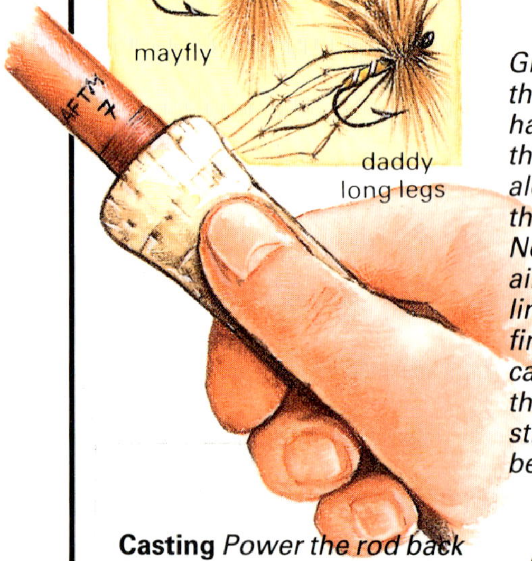

Grip the rod near the front of the handle with your thumb resting along the top of the rod butt. Never try to airialise too much line when you are first learning to cast. Practise throwing a straight line before trying for distance.

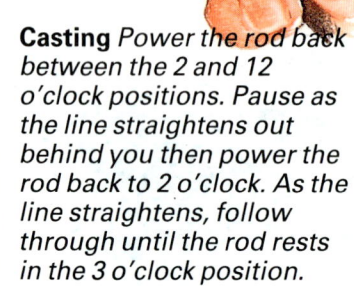

Casting Power the rod back between the 2 and 12 o'clock positions. Pause as the line straightens out behind you then power the rod back to 2 o'clock. As the line straightens, follow through until the rod rests in the 3 o'clock position.

Rods Carbon fly rods are now quite cheap and they are far lighter to use than a fibre glass rod. A good rod will be about 2.6 metres to 3 metres long. Rods and fly lines have a marking on them so that they can be balanced. This marking is the A.F.T.M. number. (Association of Fishing Tackle Makers) The rod and fly line must have the same A.F.T.M. rating. For the beginner, rods in the A.F.T.M. 5 to 7 range are ideal and this tackle can be used on lakes and also for river fishing.

Fly lines Fly lines are heavy and made from plastic. The weight of the fly line enables you to cast. The most popular fly lines are double taper and weight forward lines. A weight forward line helps the beginner to cast further. A double taper line is best for delicate presentation of small dry flies. The ideal combination for a beginner would be an A.F.T.M. 5 to 7 rod and a weight forward 6 floating line (W.F. 6F.).

Lures Lures are usually used with a sinking line. Most lures incorporate flashing material which catches the light encouraging the trout to grab them. Lures are most suitable for use on lakes and reservoirs.

A common problem when casting a fly is dropping the rod too far back on the back cast. The line will either catch on the grass or land in a heap on the forward cast.

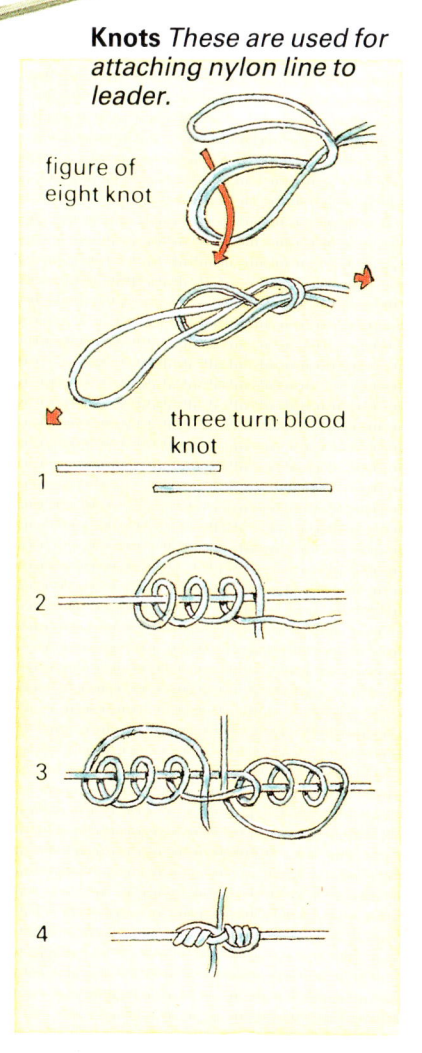

Knots These are used for attaching nylon line to leader.

figure of eight knot

three turn blood knot

Sticking the rod butt up the sleeve of your jacket on your casting arm stops you going too far back on your back cast.

13

FLY FISHING 2

BROWN TROUT FISHING

The brown trout usually comes into season in March, although it varies in different areas. The water temperature at this time of year is often very low and the trout tend to be lying deep. To get the fly down to these trout make a paste from Fullers earth and washing up liquid to rub along the nylon leader. This degreases the line, which helps to break the surface of the water so the fly sinks quickly. In very deep sections of river a leaded fly will work best. Cast upstream and across so that by the time your fly is level with you it has sunk to the required depth. As the water temperature rises during the later months then a dry fly fished upstream and across will catch a lot of trout.

GRAYLING FISHING

Grayling live in the same types of river as trout. Unlike trout, they form shoals and it is possible to get a good catch of grayling from one swim. The best time to fish for grayling is from September onwards. Grayling are naturally bottom feeders but they will rise readily to a dry fly. A rising grayling will swim up vertically from the river bottom, take the fly and then dive back to take up its position near the river bed. If your tackle is too clumsy the fish will turn away from the fly at the last moment. When they do this it is termed 'coming short' and the cure is to use a finer leader and smaller fly.

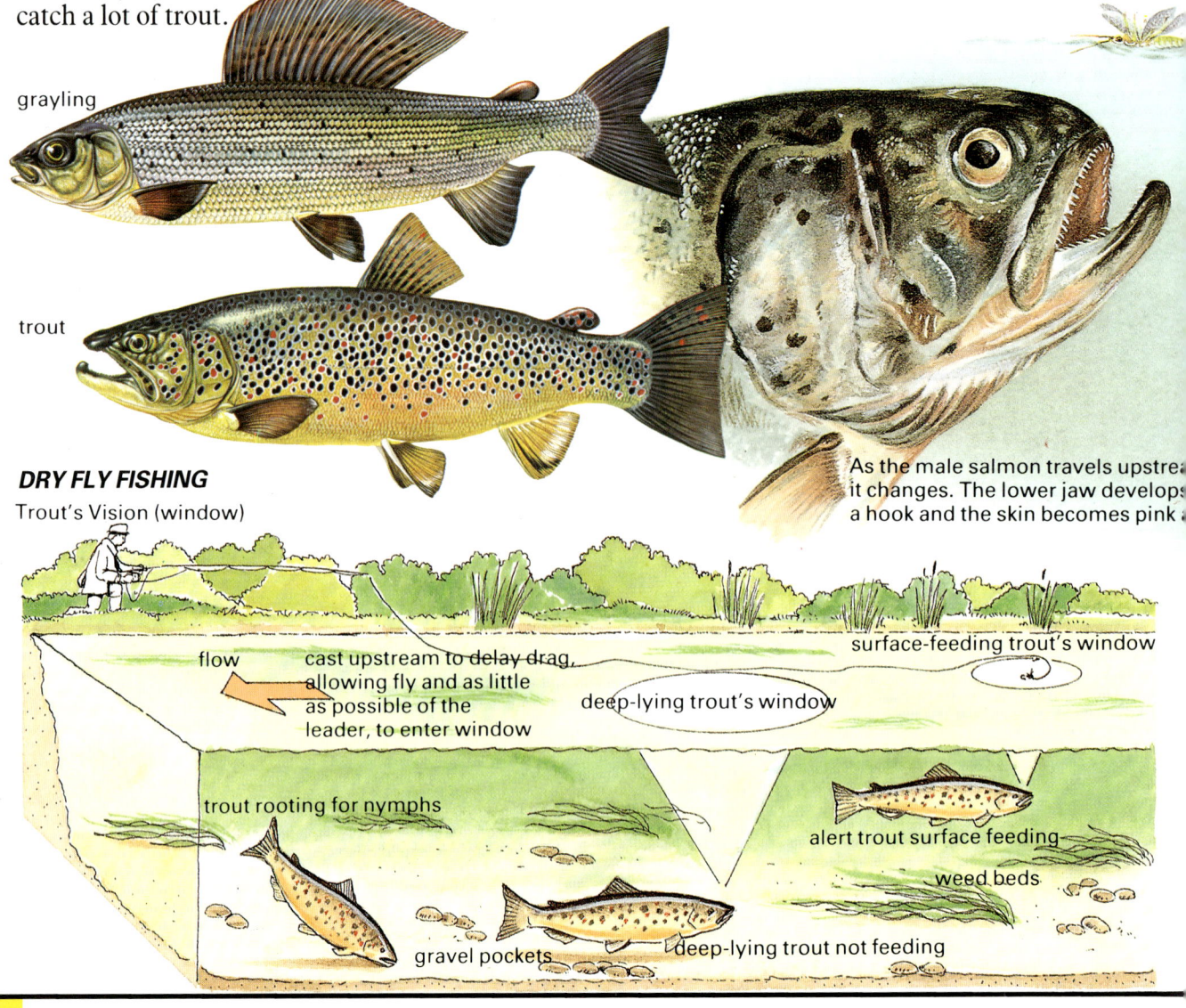

grayling

trout

As the male salmon travels upstream it changes. The lower jaw develops a hook and the skin becomes pink

DRY FLY FISHING

Trout's Vision (window)

flow

cast upstream to delay drag, allowing fly and as little as possible of the leader, to enter window

surface-feeding trout's window

deep-lying trout's window

trout rooting for nymphs

alert trout surface feeding

weed beds

gravel pockets

deep-lying trout not feeding

14

WADING

Most trout reaches of rivers are fast flowing, shallow and rocky and it is often necessary, therefore, to wade into the river to cast to rising trout. Great care should be taken when wading, for not only can the bottom of the river be very slippery, but also noisy wading will scare away the fish. If you have to wade to cast to rising trout and grayling, do so very slowly and carefully. A short-handled flip-up landing net is very useful for landing trout and grayling when you are wading. When not in use the net can be clipped to your belt.

LOCATING FISH

Most trout waters are a series of pools with fast, broken water at the head of the pool, and a deep smooth section shallowing off to a glide at the end of the pool. In the early months of the year most of the trout will be found in the deeper water at the centre of the pool where the broken water begins to iron out into a smooth glide. As the water temperature rises, the trout will move into the faster, broken water at the head of the pool where there is more oxygen. The shallow tail of the pool is where the fish will drop to in the evening to intercept dry flies.

In squally, windy weather, trout will often rise, feeding well on the surface of the water, following the wind lanes. In such conditions, trout will often cruise upwind in large groups.

CASTING FROM A FIXED POSITION

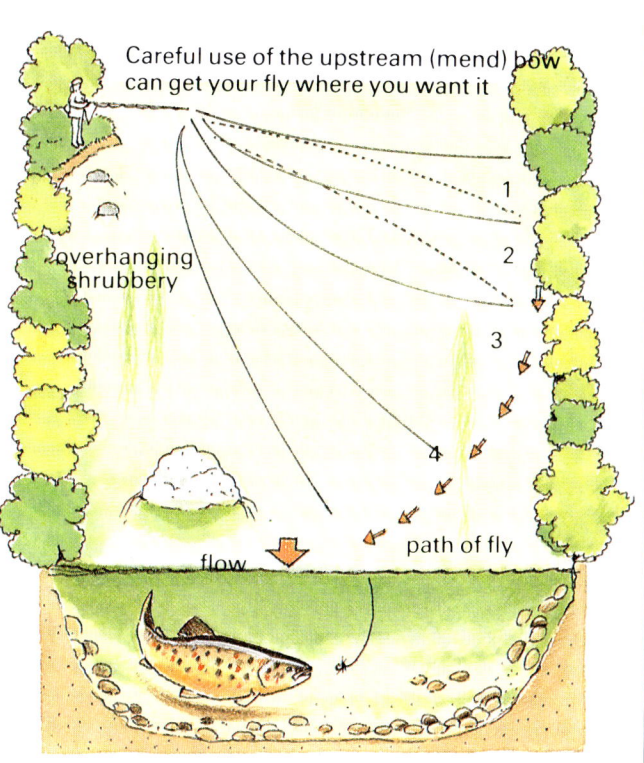

Careful use of the upstream (mend) bow can get your fly where you want it

overhanging shrubbery

path of fly
flow

In clear water, trout which have been spotted lying near the river bed can be induced to take a fly even if they are not really feeding. Cast a leaded fly upstream and as it approaches the trout, lift the rod tip smoothly so that the fly suddenly moves across the trout's line of vision. Even a non-feeding trout will lunge at the fly instinctively and is hooked before it realises what is happening.

WET FLY FISHING

angler kneeling for concealment

The Induced Take

flow

lightly greased leader

nymph lifted

lifted rod causes nymph to dip and often induces trout to take

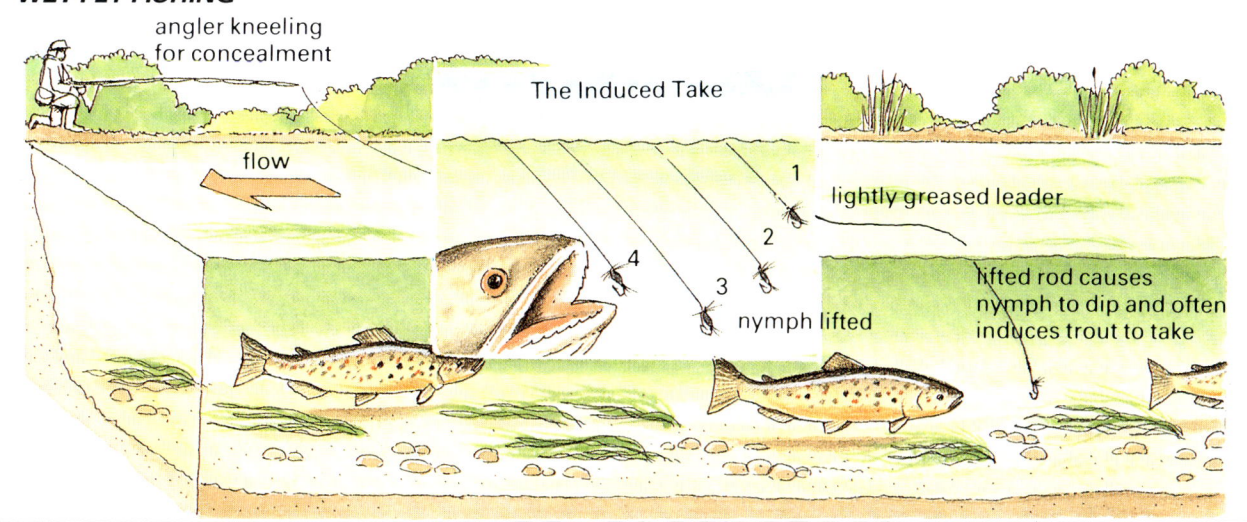

LEGERING

Legering is the method used for catching fish on or near the bottom of a lake or river without using a float. In most instances, the bait is held in position on the river bed by a heavy weight attached to the line. This method is often used by anglers trying to catch larger specimens of each species of fish. Larger baits can be presented easily on leger tackle and left in one place long enough for bigger fish to find the bait. When a fish picks up the bait, it draws the line taut to the rod; there are several types of bait indicator that can be attached to the rod which signal a bite very effectively.

Swim feeders
Swim feeders are used for holding the bait in position on the river bed and releasing ground bait into the swim (or area you are fishing) at the same time. In its simplest form it is a weighted rubber tube open at both ends with holes drilled in the tube wall.

Closed feeder
This is simply a tube with a cap at both ends. The tube is filled with maggots and the cap replaced. On the riverbed the maggots crawl out of the holes in a steady flow of loose feed.

Open ended feeder *One end is plugged with damp ground bait; maggots are then poured on top and the other end is also sealed with the damp ground bait. When the ground bait dissolves the maggots are washed around your baited hook.*

LINE LEGER TACKLE

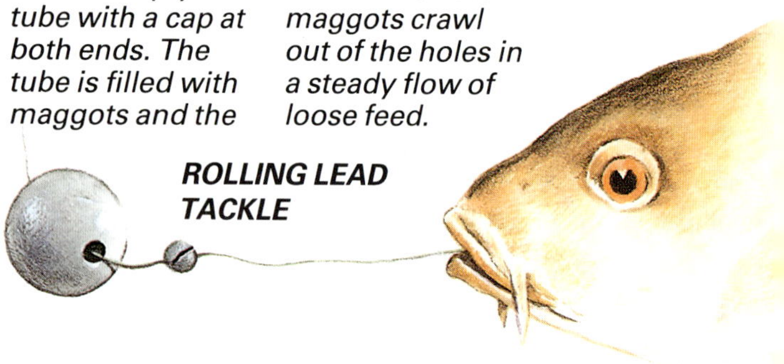

ARLESLEY BOMB TACKLE

COFFIN LEAD TACKLE

ROLLING LEAD TACKLE

SWIM FEEDERS

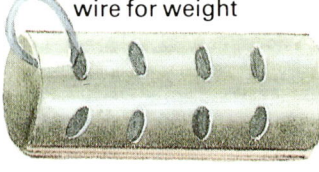

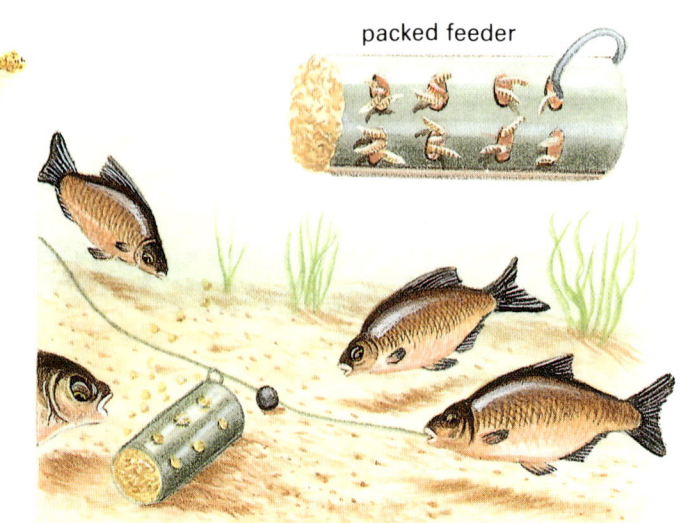

feeder with nylon loop and wrapped wire for weight

packed feeder

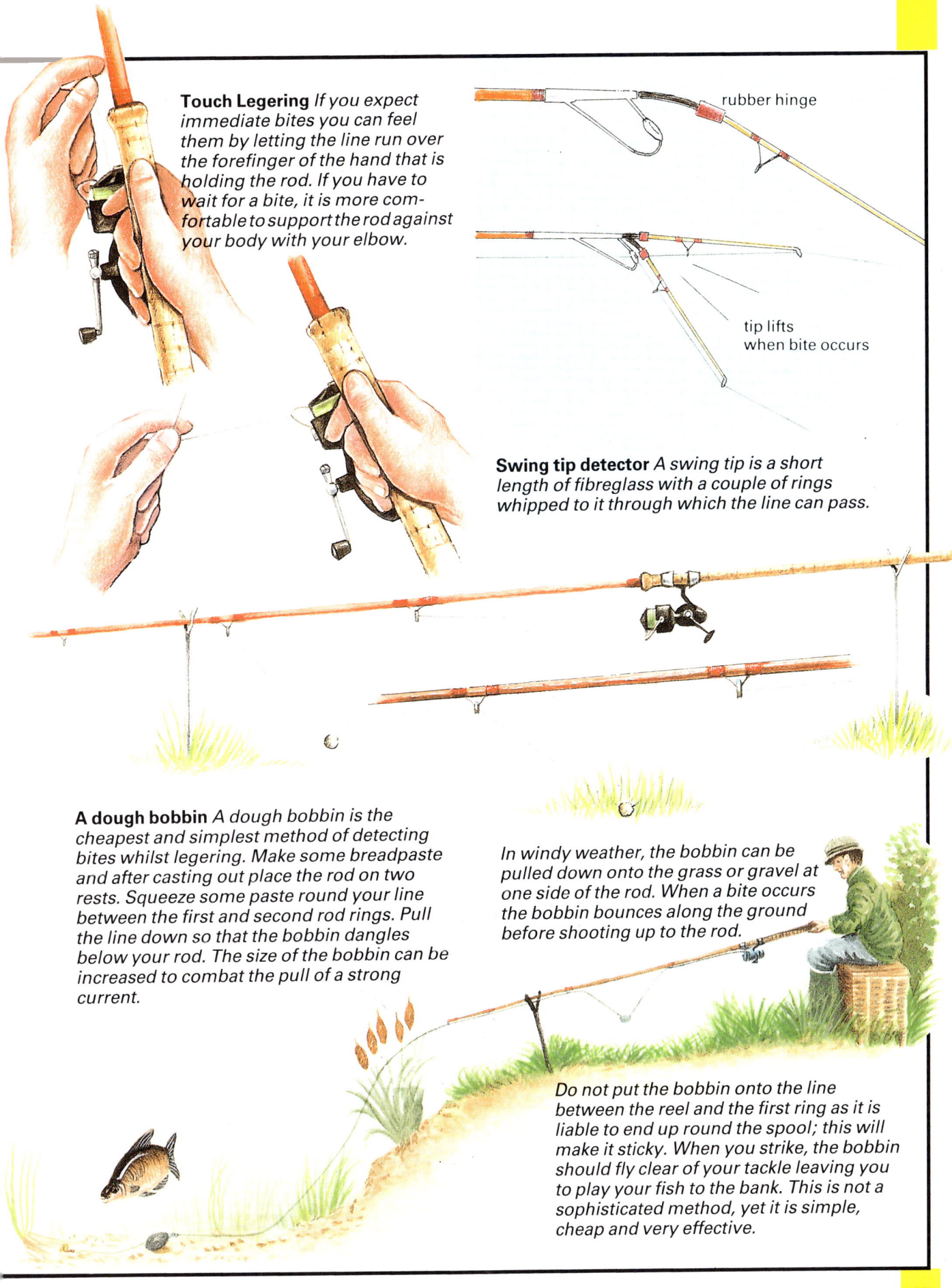

Touch Legering If you expect immediate bites you can feel them by letting the line run over the forefinger of the hand that is holding the rod. If you have to wait for a bite, it is more comfortable to support the rod against your body with your elbow.

rubber hinge

tip lifts when bite occurs

Swing tip detector A swing tip is a short length of fibreglass with a couple of rings whipped to it through which the line can pass.

A dough bobbin A dough bobbin is the cheapest and simplest method of detecting bites whilst legering. Make some breadpaste and after casting out place the rod on two rests. Squeeze some paste round your line between the first and second rod rings. Pull the line down so that the bobbin dangles below your rod. The size of the bobbin can be increased to combat the pull of a strong current.

In windy weather, the bobbin can be pulled down onto the grass or gravel at one side of the rod. When a bite occurs the bobbin bounces along the ground before shooting up to the rod.

Do not put the bobbin onto the line between the reel and the first ring as it is liable to end up round the spool; this will make it sticky. When you strike, the bobbin should fly clear of your tackle leaving you to play your fish to the bank. This is not a sophisticated method, yet it is simple, cheap and very effective.

Rivers 1

Most rivers can be divided into three different zones. The rocky upper reaches of a river where the current is fast-flowing, supports mostly trout and grayling, although a few chub and dace may also be found.

The middle reaches of a river are usually the best fisheries. Trout will still be present but the water will also support most species of coarse fish. Here, the river can vary from fast-flowing gravelly pools to slow, deep, willow-lined glides.

In the lower reaches of the river there is a steady flow and the river is usually wide with often featureless banks. Few if any trout will be found in these reaches; bream, roach and chub will be the dominant species. Bream and roach will be found right down to the tidal reaches of the river.

Perch prefer the slower reaches of a river. Clear gaps between weedbeds are good places to look for river perch.

The shallow margins near the edge of rivers will attract hordes of minnows and coarse fish fry during the summer months. Large fish will venture onto these shallows at night to feed on the smaller fish.

Minnows prefer clean, shallow, well-oxygenated water and will congregate in thousands in river margins in summer.

Barbel will move and feed in the most turbulent part of a river even under the sill of a weirpool. At night, they will feed in very shallow glides where there is a sandy or gravelly bed.

The gravelly run-offs at the end of weirpools are favourite places to find barbel and gudgeon. Both species love well-oxygenated water flowing over a fine gravel bed.

Gudgeon are to be found where the river bed is fine gravel or sand. They prefer a good flow but in winter will drop into deeper, slower water.

Chub *are very fond of cover and will lie up under trailing branches. At night they will often venture into shallower water.*

Submerged roots from riverside willows and alders provide sanctuary for many fish. Chub especially, will take up position against overhanging willow bushes.

chub

minnows

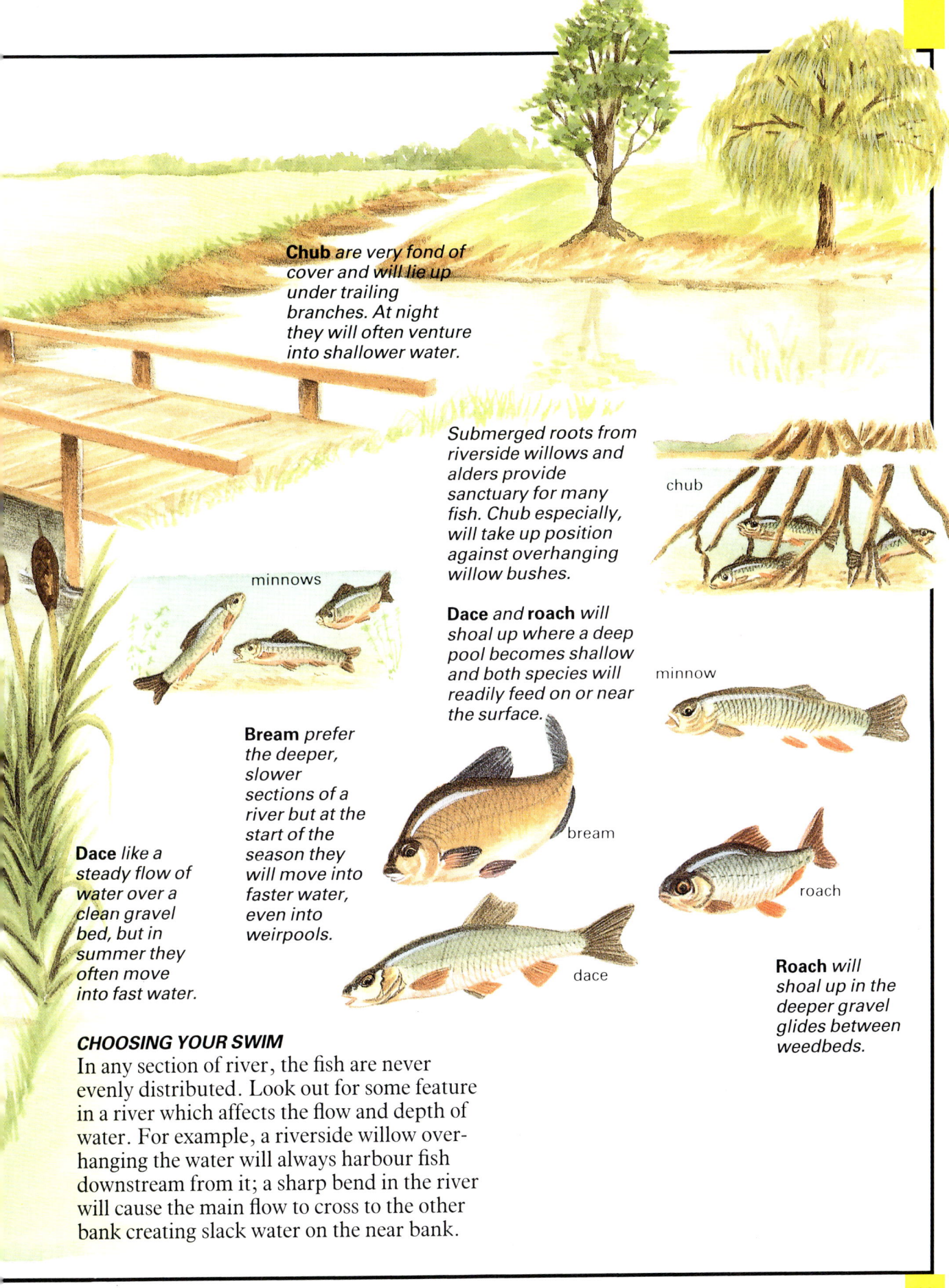

Dace *and* **roach** *will shoal up where a deep pool becomes shallow and both species will readily feed on or near the surface.*

minnow

Bream *prefer the deeper, slower sections of a river but at the start of the season they will move into faster water, even into weirpools.*

bream

roach

Dace *like a steady flow of water over a clean gravel bed, but in summer they often move into fast water.*

dace

Roach *will shoal up in the deeper gravel glides between weedbeds.*

CHOOSING YOUR SWIM

In any section of river, the fish are never evenly distributed. Look out for some feature in a river which affects the flow and depth of water. For example, a riverside willow overhanging the water will always harbour fish downstream from it; a sharp bend in the river will cause the main flow to cross to the other bank creating slack water on the near bank.

19

Rivers 2

The most widely-used floats for fishing a flowing river are a stick float or an avon float. The avon float has a more bulky body and is used for carrying a large amount of shot to hold the bait down in a heavy current.

When you are trotting a float down a river you are better standing up to fish. By doing so you have far greater control over your tackle and will find it much easier to mend your line as the current puts a bow in it.

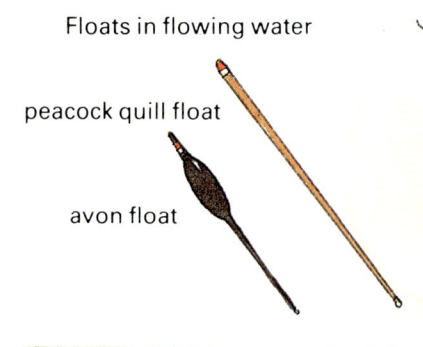

Floats in flowing water
peacock quill float
avon float

When fished at the speed of the current the float will always travel ahead of the bait. This is because the current is faster on the surface than on the bottom of a river.

In a river with beds of streamer weed, trot the float down the gullies between the weedbeds.

When a fish intercepts the bait, the force of the current pushing the float under the surface indicates a bite.

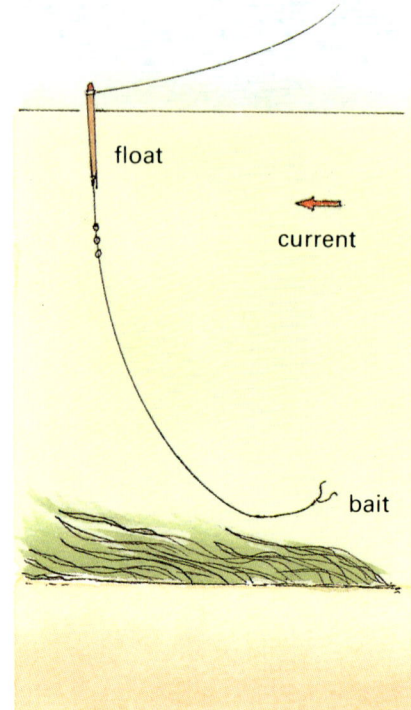

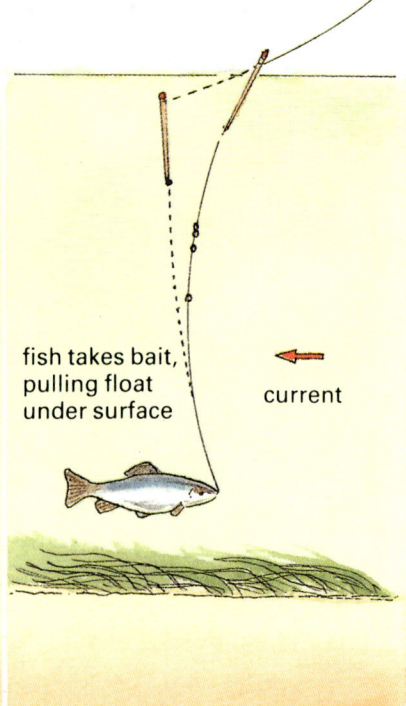

float
current
bait

fish takes bait, pulling float under surface
current

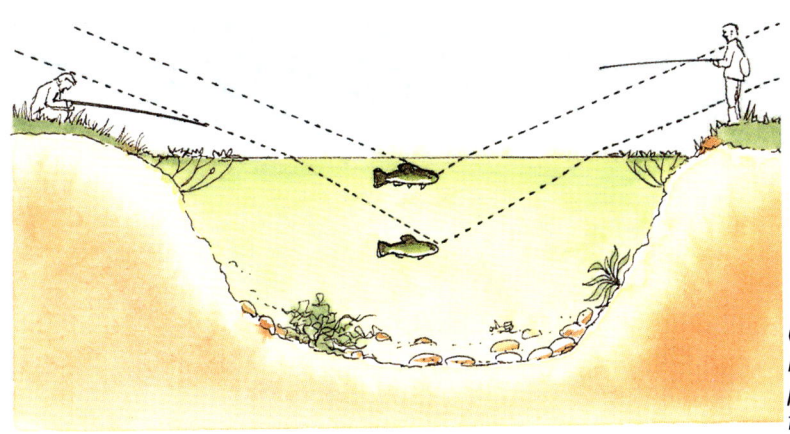

A fish's eye view The deeper a fish lies, the better view of the bank it has. A crouching or sitting angler is less likely to be spotted than a standing one.

On a wide, clear river, it is often possible to trot a float very long distances. When striking at long range, swing the rod well back to ensure the hook is driven home.

Introduce small amounts of maggots and casters into your swim by throwing them upstream. Don't forget to allow for the speed of the current so that your groundbait reaches the bottom in your swim. Loose feed should be introduced on a 'little and often' basis. A few maggots thrown in at every cast is better than several handfuls thrown in all at once.

Stret pegging In this method, the float is set over depth with the shot lying on the river bed. Cast downstream and tighten up. By raising and lowering the rod tip, the bait can be inched slowly through the swim. This is a good tactic to employ for fishing a river that is running high.

When your float has travelled to the end of your swim, hold back for a minute so that your bait rises up from the bottom. This often induces a fish to take.

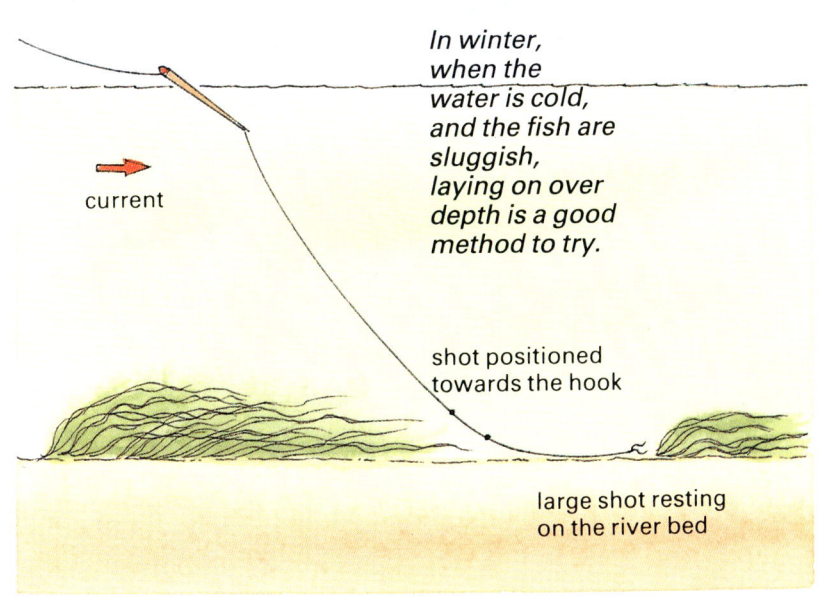

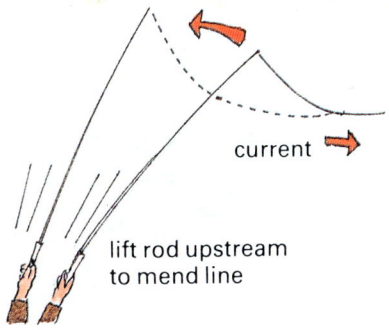

In winter, when the water is cold, and the fish are sluggish, laying on over depth is a good method to try.

current

shot positioned towards the hook

large shot resting on the river bed

current

lift rod upstream to mend line

21

LAKES, PONDS AND GRAVEL PITS 1

Even the smallest farm pond can provide good fishing, and with so much pressure from competing interests such as boating, for large areas of water, small lakes and ponds now provide some of the best sport. Some lakes are extremely easy to fish whereas others can be very difficult.

When fishing a lake spend some time walking round and studying the different features which may affect the fish life. It is also a good idea to spend some time plumbing the depth around the lake so that you understand the contours of the lake bed. Find out where the bottom is muddy and where it is hard and gravelly. Plants are often an indication of this. Reedmace, a tall plant with cigar-shaped seed heads grows in mud, whereas the true bulrush, with its tall, dark green stems, prefers a gravelly bottom. Avoid deep, smelly mud where debris collects.

Lily pads *Many species, especially carp and pike will lie amongst the shade of lily pads. Lilies have very tough stems and it is unwise to try and catch fish from the middle of a bed of lilies. The chances are you will only leave a fish tangled up or trailing a length of line.*

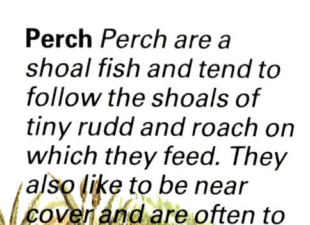

Perch *Perch are a shoal fish and tend to follow the shoals of tiny rudd and roach on which they feed. They also like to be near cover and are often to be found by submerged trees and branches. Large gaps between weedbeds are also good places to fish. Float-fished worm is an excellent method for catching perch.*

Pike *During the warmer months of the year pike will lurk wherever there is cover. They can be spotted lying motionless near lily pads or weeds. In winter, pike tend to congregate in deeper water where they follow shoals of small roach and bream.*

Tench Tench are early morning or late evening feeders. Look for an area where fine silt lies over a gravelly bottom. Balls of fine ground bait laced with maggots can be introduced before fishing. The maggots crawl into the silt and the tench attracted by the ground bait will spend hours rooting in the mud to extract the maggots. Set the float so the bait is just clear of the bed.

Roach Small roach can be caught almost anywhere and at any time. The larger roach, like tench, tend to feed best in failing light. The smaller fish can be taken fishing on the drop so that the bait sinks slowly through the water. Breadflake is an excellent bait for larger roach.

Eels Eels prefer to lie up near snags such as sunken trees and undercut banks. They are largely nocturnal creatures. Legered lobworms or small dead fish are the best tactics for catching eels.

Bream Small skimmer bream can often be found shoaling amongst the roach. A large feeding shoal of bream will cause the water to colour up in a shallow lake as they grub up the bottom for food.

Rudd In waters where they are found, rudd tend to be very prolific. They are harder fighters than roach and thus provide excellent sport. They are midwater to surface feeders. Breadflake, maggots or redworms are the best baits to use.

Carp During the summer months carp will cruise around just under the surface or gather in small groups hanging motionless under overhanging branches. Carp, like bream, feeding on the bed of a lake will cause the water to become cloudy as they stir up the mud. They will often heave themselves clear of the surface. One of the most enjoyable methods of catching carp is with floating crust.

LAKES, PONDS AND GRAVEL PITS 2

Gravel pits are the water-filled lagoons left when the ground has been excavated to produce gravel and hardcore for roadbuilding and they are, without doubt, the fisheries of the future. They can vary in size from only a few acres to hundreds of acres. Before they mature and the banks become vegetated they can appear very barren and featureless. The water in gravel pits is usually of a very high quality and is often crystal clear. Once the pits are stocked and the fish become established they can grow to tremendous sizes. The largest roach, tench, bream, carp and pike in recent years have all been caught in gravel pits.

Knowledge of the depths and light and shade in the area you are fishing will help you locate fish at different times of the day.

Margin fishing *In lakes where there is no bankside disturbance, fish will feed very close to the margins. Even on lakes where the banks are disturbed by walkers, picnickers and anglers, the fish will often venture very close to the bank in the evening and feed there until well after dawn.*

You have to keep very quiet to catch these margin feeding fish. Sit well back from the water's edge and don't keep standing up or stamping about.

overhanging shrubs

tree roots

a) sheltered area for late evening gathering

b) fish congregate on clay banks in daytime

c) shallow water in warm sunny conditions is favoured for feeding

carp

The catapult
Groundbaiting at long range can be difficult, yet accuracy is very important. The easiest way to ensure this, is to take a boat out and put the groundbait in the right spot. If this is not possible, the next best method is to use a strong groundbait catapult. The pouch should be big enough to take golf ball-sized groundbait balls. Maggots can be introduced by mixing them in groundbait.

Groundbaiting
Groundbaiting is very important in a gravel pit especially for species such as carp and bream. It is a good idea to prebait an area several days prior to fishing. Lay trails of groundbait along a shelf to one main area. When you do prebait and begin to fish, don't lose heart if you don't start catching straight away. Sooner or later fish will move over the baited area.

LOCATING FISH IN GRAVEL PITS
The depth of gravel pits can vary enormously and the bottom is seldom even across the area. In a recently matured pit where the water is clear, by standing on a high bank, it is possible to pinpoint the deeper areas, as the water looks darker. Fish tend to stay in the deeper water during the daytime and at night venture up the shelves onto the shallow gravel spits to feed. The shelves and ledges which form the boundary between very deep and very shallow water are good areas on which to concentrate. Islands have been left in some gravel pits to form breeding sanctuaries for wildfowl, and the edges of these are often worth fishing even if it means long casting.

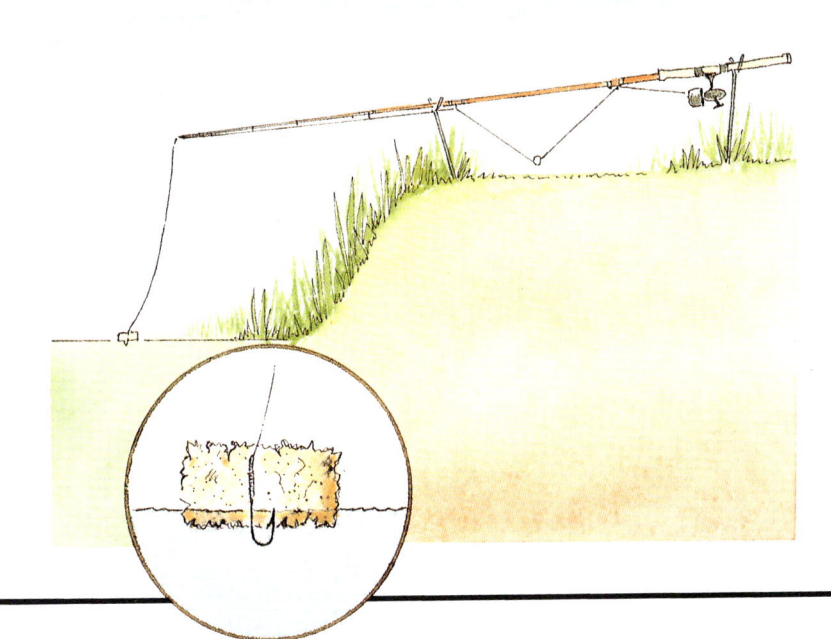

Carp will take floating crust fished right against the bank. If the bank is steep and undercut, set a dough bobbin indicator on the line, so that you know when a carp has taken the crust.

Cut out a cube of crust from an unsliced loaf and press the hook through the crust so that the hook is hidden by the soft flake.

CANALS

In general, canals do not make very good fisheries. The main reason for this is the amount of boat traffic. In recent years, pleasure craft have taken over from commercial traffic as the main users of canals, to such an extent that fishing can be almost continually interrupted.

A canal should be tackled in a similar fashion to a small still water, but tackle needs to be much finer. Most of the fish you catch in a canal will be small gudgeon, roach and skimmer bream. Some canals have been stocked with carp and tench. Hook lengths need to be very fine and the hooks very small – a size 20 or 24 for a single caster or bloodworm.

BAITS
The three most successful baits on a canal are caster, bloodworm and breadflake. During the winter, canals can be very clear and extremely difficult to fish. Groundbait very sparingly. Bloodworm can be found in the mud at the bottom of ponds and canals or they can be bought from some tackle dealers or obtained by mail order.

Eels Eels abound in canals and provide an opportunity to catch a decent-sized fish. Float fished worm is the best method of catching them. Choose a spot near a walled bank or near lock gates for your fishing.

Unhook your eel in the water with a pair of artery forceps to save getting slime on your hands.

WEIRPOOLS

Big weirpools, such as those on the rivers Thames and Trent, are excellent places to fish. The well-oxygenated water and the snags that are often found in a weirpool attract many fish. Barbel are the most usual fish to catch in weirpools and they will lie right up under the sill of the weir where the water is white and foaming. As the light fades in the evening, barbel will drop back to the shallow tail of the weirpool to feed over the gravel bottom. Chub are the other species of fish that thrive in weirpools. At the beginning of summer, vast shoals of chub will congregate in the streaming water below the weir. They are attracted to the high oxygenation which helps them regain their strength from spawning. Pike will also sometimes collect in a weirpool to take advantage of the vast numbers of dace and small chub there. Even bream will venture into the turbulent water during the summer.

Chub Chub are a shy fish but they are also very greedy. If you fish quietly you can catch large numbers of chub from a weirpool. Float fished bread or legered crust or cheese will attract many fish. But beware! Bites from chub can be very vicious and nearly drag your rod into the river.

Barbel Barbel are the most powerful fish to be found in a river. Never fish for barbel with light tackle as it will be easily broken. They are not particularly hook-shy and will accept a big bait. Legered worm, luncheon meat or a bunch of maggots will catch barbel. Don't be afraid to cast into the very turbulent water against the weir sill even if you have to have a large leger to hold bottom.

Seasons

Fish are cold-blooded creatures and their activity is dictated by water temperatures and weather conditions. During the winter all fish are less active and some species, notably carp and tench, become very sluggish indeed. During the winter, fish will tend to move to deeper water where it is slightly warmer. Feeding spells will be shorter and smaller baits will be taken in preference to large ones.

COLD WATER FLOAT FISHING

In winter, when the surface of a lake is flat and calm and the water clear and cold, it can be very difficult to catch fish. Set up an antenna float with a very slender tip. Shot the float so that only the slightest bit of the tip is showing above the surface. Set the depth so that the bait is only just clear of the lake bed. Caster is a better bait than maggot in cold water. Bites will be positive but the float will just sink and stay there.

It is very important to keep warm. A large fishing umbrella tilted behind you will keep a cold wind off your back as well as keeping you dry. In really windy weather, remember to stake the umbrella down with guy ropes to prevent it blowing away.

In windy weather, use an antenna float and submerge the rod tip to overcome surface drift.

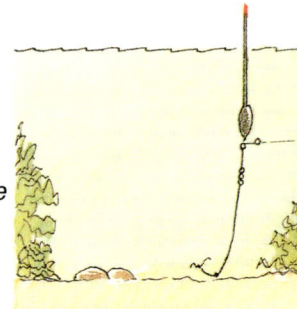

The antenna float
This has a bulbous body and a long narrow stem and is ideal for stillwater fishing. Some shot should be resting on the bed with all the other shot well up the line. In gusty weather, undershotting (below) ensures that more of the float can be seen.

Angler's code

Angling clubs have a set of rules which all members must obey. These rules are designed to protect a fishery and to ensure that most anglers can enjoy their day's fishing without interfering with the enjoyment of others. The environment must also be protected. Considerate behaviour at the waterside not only preserves the good relationship the club has with riverbank dwellers but will also help you catch more fish. Noisy behaviour along the riverbank will upset serious anglers and also scare away the fish. Always approach the water and tackle up quietly.

Do not smash down rushes and other vegetation if the banks are overgrown. Folding over a few rush stems in order to fish is perfectly in order but destroying all the tall vegetation with a landing net handle will be viewed as vandalism. Always respect any farm land you pass through. Leave gates open or closed as you have found them, unless it is obvious someone else has left a gate open and livestock have escaped. A farmer who finds his herd of cattle in his wheat field will not be very pleased. Never light fires on the riverbank.

FISH HANDLING

Always treat your fish with care. Make sure your hands are wet and handle the fish as little as possible. The slime on a fish's body protects it from fungal infections. Stake your keepnet out in the water so that the rings don't fold over themselves. Place fish gently into the net; never throw them in. Big fish such as carp, barbel and pike are best returned straight to the water rather than retained in the net. Release other fish at the end of the day by lowering the mouth of the net into the water. Lift the bottom of the net and let the fish swim away.

Landing your fish *Small fish may be swung out to hand but larger fish have to be netted. When the hooked fish shows signs of tiring, sink the landing net into the water. When the fish is played out, raise the rod and draw the fish over the sunken net and then lift it. If the fish is exceptionally large, you can then lay the rod on a rest and lift it out with both hands.*

IMPORTANT WARNING
Several anglers have been killed or badly injured when fishing with carbon rods under electric power lines. Electricity can arc to the rod tip without the rod even touching the cables. Another danger area is a big weir-pool. However tempting it is, do not walk along the narrow sill of a weir pool. If you slip off into the pool, the water is usually deep with very strong undercurrents.

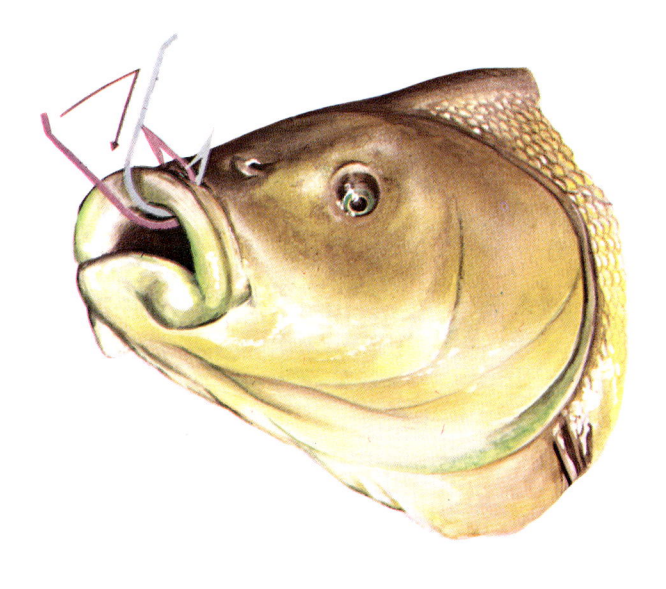

When unhooking a fish, gently ease the hook clear of the mouth and press back towards the tail.

A disgorger should be used to remove the barb from a deeply hooked fish.

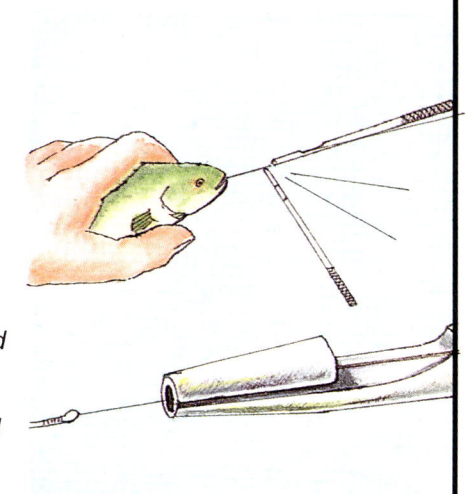

HAZARDS

One of the biggest hazards to wildlife at the waterside is nylon discarded by thoughtless anglers. Never leave nylon mesh or netting lying about on the bank as birds and animals will become entangled in it and will often die. A still greater crime is to leave a length of nylon with a baited hook on the end. A dead robin dangling from a tree on a length of nylon will not win anglers many friends. There is no excuse for leaving litter of any description at the waterside and if you find any litter already there, pick it up and take it home.

WATER POLLUTION

Sadly, a lot of industrial waste and sewage is still discharged into our river systems. Silage run off from farms is also a serious threat to our rivers and lakes. Anglers are usually amongst the first people to notice that pollution has occurred. If you find any dead fish, or notice that the colour of the water has changed over a period, then notify the local water authority and your club officials. The telephone number of your water authority is on your fishing licence.

Several very effective baits are sold in tin cans. Sweet corn and luncheon meat are perhaps the most well known. Open the tins at home and take the bait with you in plastic bait boxes. This will not only save having to fumble with a tin opener on the river bank but more importantly will prevent any tins being left on the bankside. The jagged edges of tin cans can not only maim farm animals but there are also several instances of anglers themselves being very badly cut by tin cans discarded in long grass.

Care should be taken when weighing a big fish. Special weighing nets can be bought or made. A cheap and effective method is to place the fish in a large plastic shopping bag. Fishmongers and butchers have scales with a hook attachment. The hook on the scales can be passed through the bag handles. The bag is so light it can be ignored on the scales.

Index

angler's code 30
antenna float 29

bait 3, 20, 26, 31
barbel 4, 18, 27
bream 4, 18, 23, 30

canals 26
carp 4, 22, 23, 25, 28, 30
casting 6, 7, 12, 15
catapult 25
chub 4, 18
closed feeder 16

dace 4, 18
deadbaiting 10, 11
dough bobbin 17
dry fly fishing 14

equipment 2, 3

feeders 16, 17
fish; species of 4, 5; habitats of 18, 19
fishing: coarse 8; cold water float 8, 28; fly 12–15

Fishing Tackle Makers, Association of (AFTM) 13
floats 8, 20, 29

gravel pits 25
groundbaiting 25
gudgeon 18

handling fish 30

lead tackle 16
legering 16, 17, 27
line 3; fly 13; nylon 31
lure 13

maggots 3, 21, 28
minnow 18

perch 5, 18, 22
pike 5, 22, 27, 30
pike gag 11
ponds 22–25

reel 2, 12; spool 6
rivers 18–21

rod; carbon 3, 13; leger 2; match or floating 2
rudd 23

shot 2
sink and draw method 11
spinning 10
stret pegging 21
striking 11
swim feeders 16
swing tip detector 17

tench 5, 23, 28
trotting 9, 20, 21
trout 14, 15, 18

wading 15
waggler float 8
water pollution 31
weighing catch 31
weirpools 27, 30

zander 4

Useful glossary

Arlesey bomb Pear-shaped leger weight.
Artery forceps Pincers for removing large hooks from a fish's mouth.
Bobbin indicator A device for detecting bites whilst legering.
Bread baits Crust, flakes or paste made from bread and used as bait.
Breaking strain A manufacturer's estimate of the dry strength of the line. It decreases when wet, knotted or old.
Close season Season when fishing for coarse fish is not allowed.
Coarse fish Freshwater fish not belonging to the salmon or trout family. Such fish cannot usually be eaten.
Deadbaiting Fishing for predatory fish with dead fish as bait.
Disgorger A tool for removing the hook from a fish's mouth.
Dry fly An artificial fly fished on a greased line so that it floats on the water surface.
Float fishing Method of presenting a bait suspended below a float.
Fly fishing Fishing with an artificial fly usually in pursuit of game fish such as trout or salmon.
Game fish Fish, usually trout or salmon, which can be eaten.
Groundbait Bait used to attract fish to the swim and to encourage them to feed.
Laying on Method of presenting a stationary bait in a flowing river with float tackle. The float is adjusted so that the tackle is fished well over depth.
Legering A method of fishing where the bait lies on the water's bed and lead weights hold the tackle in position.
Over depth The depth of water is less than the distance between float and hook.
Quiver tip Sensitive bite indicator attached to the top of the rod.
Mepps spinner Type of revolving artificial lure.
Nymphs Wet flies, simulating larval or pupal forms of insects.
Spinner Revolving artificial line used for catching predatory fish.
Stret pegging Like laying on, the float is set to fish over depth and a large shot is placed near the hook so that it is lying on the river bed.
Swim Term given to the area of water being fished.
Swing tip Bite indicator attached to the rod and used when legering.
Swivel Swivels and anti-kink vanes are devices used to prevent lines twisting or kinking when spinning or legering.
Trace A length of nylon or wire attached to the reel line.
Trotting A form of float fishing where the float and tackle is allowed to travel down with the stream.
Wet fly An artificial fly which is fished below the water surface.

Published in 1989 by
The Hamlyn Publishing Group Limited
Michelin House, 81 Fulham Road, London SW3 6RB

Copyright © The Hamlyn Publishing Group Limited 1989
All rights reserved. No part of this publication may be reproduced, stored in a retrieval system, or transmitted in any form or by any means, electronic, mechanical, photocopying, recording or otherwise, without the prior permission of The Hamlyn Publishing Group Limited.

ISBN 0 600 56324 3

Printed and bound in Italy
Front jacket illustrations: Brian Morland and Roy Westwood

Photographs: Brian Morland
Illustrations: Simon Burr
Design: David Robinson